COMMUNICATING

FROM THE INSIDE

OUT

Revised Printing

It's about taking exposed btw different culture

Barbara Bullard
Kat Carroll
Orange Coast College

Claires
Jewelry

KENDALL/HUNT PUBLISHING COMPANY
4050 Westmark Drive   Dubuque, Iowa 52002

CONTENTS

Unit One: Beginning the Journey

Chapter One: Becoming an Explorer

Chapter Two: Discovering Who We Are

Chapter Three: Perceiving a New You

Chapter Four: The New Frontier

Unit Two: Further Explorations

Chapter Five: Self-Talk As A Key To Change

Chapter Six: Visualizing New Territory

Chapter Seven: Discovering the "Whole" You

Chapter Eight: Listening to Your Inner Guidance

Chapter Nine: The World Is Yours

Unit Three: Activities for Self-Discovery

Section One: Self-Concept, Self-Image, Self-Esteem

Section Two: Internal Process

ACKNOWLEDGMENTS

Dan Carr	Illustrations
Alden Barry	Cover Art
Rahel Schwartz	Photography
Scott Morse	Photography

DEDICATION

To the Positive Pygmalions who have inspired us during the journey:

Dr. Owen Jenson, who stands before his students and opens the doors of perception for those who have the courage to enter.

Our mothers, **Vivian Grant** and **Barbara Kirkendall,** who taught us to be true to ourselves and dared us to embark on the road less traveled.

Our husbands, **Jay Bullard** and **Dick Carroll,** who have passionately and patiently shared this journey with us.

UNIT ONE
Beginning the Journey

Chapter One
BECOMING AN EXPLORER

ATTITUDES FOR LEARNING

(adj) healthy mind

*There is, in sanest hours, a consciousness, a thought that rises,
independent, lifted out from all else, calm, like the stars, shining
eternal.* *(adj)*   *(n)* *bất diệt*

*This is the thought of identity—yours for you, whoever you are,
as mine for me...*

                                        Walt Whitman

lôn xộn
phức tạp   *bao la*

   We live our lives in an intricate, complex world, so immense that we can neve
consciously learn everything currently known about it. As much as we know abou
this wonderful planet today, new mysteries are continually unfolding. In fact, b
tomorrow some of the information that was discovered yesterday will be obsolete
This thought excites many people who will meet the earth's challenges becaus
they are true adventurers who live their lives exploring it's mysteries.

   We are not unlike the earth. We are an equally complex "world." With eac
passing day inquisitive people, who have dedicated their lives to the expansion c
human potential, map the physical, mental and emotional mysteries of the huma
race. Will we ever know everything about "who we are?" The answer can onl
begin with you, for true awareness begins with your willingness to venture into th
mysterious world of your own being. This critical step in human development i
being taken everywhere we look, as Assemblyman John Vasconcellos states i
Education For What, "We get a picture of a major effort by many persons to redefir
who we are and can be, to look more into our insides, to open ourselves and brin
ourselves to the surface. We are beginning to change both our vision of ourselve
and our experience of ourselves. This is the human revolution we live amidst."
is only after you have made this choice that the riches you have to offer can b
known. In doing so we begin to learn how to communicate from the inside out.

o **overriding** (adj.) : more important than anything else.
o **cooperative** (adj) kō ŏṕ ra tiv — helpful
o **embark** (v) go onto a ship
o **forth** (adv) (out or away, or downward

Becoming an Explorer

We, as teachers and authors, join you in a journey of self *revelation* by focusing on the **whole** person. On this path we will share the many treasures and keys we have discovered on our own journeys. According to Harvard professor Dr. Howard Gardner, "an emerging sense of self proves to be a key element in the realm of the personal intelligences, one of 'overriding importance to individuals the world over.' A developed *sense of self* often appears as the *highest achievement* of human beings...." This book is our cooperative effort to share with our students and readers insights into intrapersonal and interpersonal understanding and intelligence.

THE EDUCATION OF THE "SELF"

As educators we, the authors, are dedicated to the process of personal learning. Before embarking on this journey together we feel it is important that you consider what the word "education" means. For us it means being willing to learn what your true potential is, no matter what new subject or new skill you are undertaking. It means learning how to make use of all levels of your inner resources—physical, mental and emotional. It means having the courage to look at "who you are" and change what you don't like while making the best use of your strengths. It simply means, as a member of the human race to become **self-aware** and, in doing so, to become more responsible for your participation on this planet.

Recently and fortunately, education has been focusing attention on the critical area of self awareness. Just look at how the first line of the California Education code reads, "Each child is a unique human being with unique needs, and the purpose of schooling is to enable him or her to develop their potential as a human being." **Reforming** education means providing you, as a student of life, opportunities to become a self-aware, self-esteeming individual. We need more than just the "back to basics" approach. We believe, along with Jim Olivera, that we "need six R's, reading, writing, arithmetic, self-respect, personal responsibility, and human relationships!"

Therefore, we see our role as teachers of self awareness as helping you develop a new definition in your life for the word "education." Consider this—the root word of education is **"educare,"** which means to lead forth from within. In other words, as both educators and students of life we join you and encourage you to educate your "true self" by discovering the essence of who you are on the inside. We will practice Kahlil Gibran's words:

reciprocal (adj)

Unit One: Beginning the Journey

No man can reveal to you aught *(anything)* but that which

already lies half asleep in the dawning

of your knowledge

The teacher who walks in the shadow

of the temple, among his followers

gives not of his wisdom but

rather of his faith and his

lovingness.

If his is indeed wise he does

not bid you enter the house *(offer (v))*

of his wisdom,

but rather leads you to the

threshold of your *((n) entrance)*

own mind..

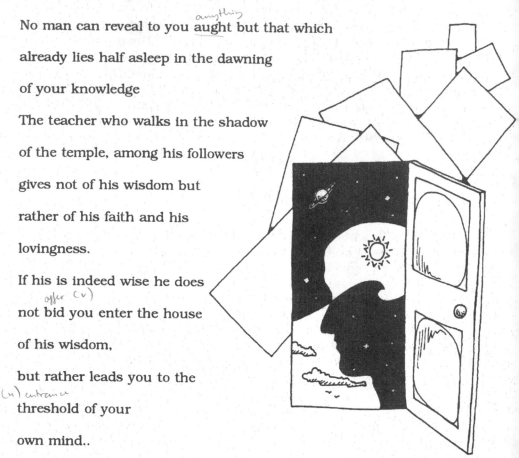

We, as educators, seek to perceive each of you as unique in your own way. A[s] communication educator Virginia Satir stated, "there is not another duplicate [of] yourself in the world, nor has there been in the 74 billion people that have com[e] before you, or the 5 billion that are here now. You are unique....you couldn['t] possibly compare yourself to anyone else."

Our promise is to share with you our discoveries, joy of learning and ou[r] passion for communicating from "the inside out." We are well aware learning an[d] growth never occur in a vacuum. Communication and education are transactiona[l,] ongoing and reciprocal. *(two-way)* Therefore, we hope and trust that YOU will ACTIVEL[Y] participate in this journey of personal discovery. Learning is an **inside job**—a[s] Gibran reminded us, no one can teach you anything without your full participatio[n.] We can only lead you to the threshold of your own mind which, like a va[st] continent, holds hidden riches just waiting to be discovered.

THE STARTING POINT OF OUR JOURNEY

Success in an ever-changing world is going to depend to a great degree on learning to understand what we have to offer as individuals and developing our skills. Your starting point, therefore, is to understand the intelligence and skills you currently possess. Dr. Gardner, a pioneer in theories of multiple intelligences, has identified six major intelligences needed for success and happiness in the future. These six areas are linguistic, logical-mathematical, spatial, musical, bodily-kinesthetic and, most interesting for our purposes, the personal intelligences of interpersonal and intrapersonal knowing. Gardner stresses that our education system has placed too much emphasis on the first four, and that present and future generations will, by necessity, need to place increasing emphasis on the "personal intelligences."

What follows are the "attitudes" we encourage you to adopt at the beginning of this journey for evolving your personal intelligences. Unlocking the doors that are the barriers to your true potential depend on your willingness to surrender old ideas about the way the world works. All of us have spent a large portion of our lives learning certain thought patterns and assumptions about the nature of our relationships, our work and our world. We have been taught by our parents, peers, educational systems, media, cultural environment and personal experiences that the world operates in a certain way. We have learned our "reality" and we interact with others based on the assumptions we have about the nature of that reality. Because these assumptions or mind-sets are often distorted by our personal perceptions, they often serve as limitations to our growth.

Many of the assumptions we make about our education are keeping the door to real learning locked. For example, as students and teachers, we "assume" that certain behaviors are called for in the classroom environment such as lecturing and note-taking. We assume certain end-results from the classroom experience such as grades and college credit. If we are only concerned about the grade, then we are limiting our own potential for growth. Consider how much more you would gain if your priority was growth and the grade was simply an extra benefit! By freeing yourself of the limitations of old assumptions you unlock limitless possibilities for new ways of thinking and of learning. Life is more than grades, college credit and paychecks. It is time to begin to unwrap the mystery of your "being."

ATTITUDINAL KEYS FOR UNLOCKING OUR POTENTIALS

What follows are a series of "new beginnings." Transformation does not happen without the willingness to change. These attitudes are new mind-sets we hope you adopt in order that you make the most of this exploration into self-awareness. They represent the willingness to transform. They can help you open the doors to your own mysteries.

Unit One: Beginning the Journey

Life Is a Classroom and It Is Time to Take the Curriculum

We often experience our lives as "frozen" moments in time with each facet of our daily routine being a separate part of the process. We go to school where we "learn." We go to work where we earn the money to pay our bills. We spend time with friends and fill our needs for being part of a group. But, we often fail to see the inter-relationship of our daily life activities. Learning a new subject or skill should not be perceived as simply a means to an end. It may be related to your work, relationships, happiness and basic self-awareness. Everything you learn has a direct consequence in the world. The very fact that you are increasing your knowledge means that you will be able to communicate differently. You are not just getting an education, you are learning how to **learn** and then allowing transformations in your attitudes, stereotypes and beliefs to interact in your relationships. Authors Gail and Terry Maul feel this shift can happen when we re-examine our definition for "learning." Their concepts include thinking more broadly about our own educational process. Learning is more than the accumulation of information. It includes the "thought in process" as well. Every interaction, encounter and judgment we make is part of the content of learning more about ourselves. As Oliver Wendel Holmes once stated, "What lies behind us and what lies before us are tiny matters compared to what lies within us."

Becoming a Risk Taker Means Facing Fears

We learn from parents, peers, the media and our own experiences that there is a lot to be afraid of in the world. Fear of rejection, ridicule and not being good enough or lovable often leads us into a paralyzed state until the fear of failure becomes a condition of learned helplessness. We may find it almost impossible to escape. For example, Tiffany, a young college student, expressed that she wasn't going to try a new experience because she wasn't already good at it. Her fear of failure was preventing her from growing, expressing and learning.

We each have the choice to live our lives as the "cowardly lion" or to become a "wizard" and find our true personhood. Life is about choice and moving beyond fear means choosing to take risks in order to move beyond our limitations. The Carnegie Foundation recently reported that the major predictor of sound mental health is an individual's willingness to risk. It is important to realize that growth implies moving out of our comfort zones and allowing for momentary confusion. that statement caused a moment of fear, stop reading and think about what it that made you afraid. Is it finding out who you are or that the journey to a better place seems frightening? Letting go of fear may not be easy. Perhaps Leo Buscaglia said it best. "Life is always an adventure, whether it is directed by love or by fear. Fear is the confining of life...the 'no.' Love is the liberating life...the 'yes.'"

8

We ask you to say "yes" to growth by letting go of your fears and memories of past failures. If we keep playing "safe," we do not grow. In exploring these new areas we encourage you to take "risks." Look upon any failure as a stepping stone to future success and personal growth. Columbus set out looking for the West Indies. We are certainly glad that, what seemed like an initial failure, became a success for millions of people who have reaped the benefits of his willingness to take risks.

"Education is an exploration. Part of it is exploration into the known. This takes place when we as teachers know and encourage students to pick routes into our familiar territory. Other times it is pure exploration into the unknown. Neither we nor the student, know what the outcomes will be."

Bob Samples, Cheryl Charles
and
Dick Barnhart

Showing up Means Choosing to Live "Now" and to Stop Avoiding Who We Are

Stepping through the door of self-awareness means living in the present. This is a new experience for many of us. Consider how many times in the course of a day you think about the past. How many of those are thoughts that are self punishing or degrading ("I never should have said that!" or "I always get involved with losers." or "I was so stupid yesterday!") keep us from dealing with who we are at the moment. We can learn a lot about negative behavior patterns from looking at our past but there is a point where we cross the line from learning about self-growth and simply begin to sound like a television re-run. Likewise, we often project our wishes, dreams and desires into the future without exercising our power by taking advantage of the moment to make them realities. We become a

Unit One: Beginning the Journey

book

sequel of one liners ("When I get rich I'm going to volunteer time to a needy cause."
or "Someday I'm going to learn how to skydive.") that sound good but don't really
motivate us to change. What we're asking you to do is muster up the courage to
look at who you are right now at this moment in time. Profound life changes can
occur when people are willing to stop avoiding themselves and learn to deal with
their "present moment realities." Martin Buber once stated "When I get to heaven
God isn't going to ask me why I wasn't Moses. He's going to ask me why I wasn't
Martin Buber." What we're asking of you is to **show up** for your life! Paying
attention is a real key to mining the buried treasures within.

You begin to live in the present when you follow these four main keys to self
growth and self discovery:

SHOW UP
PAY ATTENTION,
SPEAK YOUR INDIVIDUAL TRUTH
COMMIT YOUR ENERGIES TO GROWTH

Growth cannot occur without the first step—*showing up*. Therefore, we stress
active participation in this path of discovery—it is up to you!

A Proactive Attitude is Self-Empowering!

One of the first steps to discovering who you are is to face your fears and
take your power back! Many people live their lives as victims where they react
to all events as if they have no control. Statements such as "This always happens
to me" (instead of "I will make sure it turns out differently next time") or "She
makes me so angry" (instead of "I feel angry towards her.") or "If only things were
different" (instead of "I'm going to look at the alternatives.") communicate the
giving away of personal power. The hidden message is that the "world acts on
me, not me on it." This book is designed to help you learn how to take your power
back by becoming proactive in your life.

"Proactive," according to Stephen R. Covey, author of *7 Habits of Highly
Effective People* means that we assume responsibility for our own lives. It means
choosing our responses and being responsible for them. Being "reactive" means
empowering things outside of us with the control of our lives. Either way we are
still the ones making the decisions. The difference is a proactive person owns
it, a reactive person is owned! As we stated before, it is impossible to teach you
anything without your **active** participation. We can present you with the tools and
keys for learning but it will be up to you to choose to unlock the doors. We can create
an environment of passion and enthusiasm for the great riches to be found in this
journey of discovery, but the real choices are yours. Perhaps Gandhi said it best
when he stated "They cannot take away our self respect if we do not give it to
them." We ask you to take your self-respect back through proactive self-awareness

10

Becoming an Explorer

Become the Master of Your Life

We believe that happiness and understanding are an **inside** job. It is not the responsibility of other people to create joy in our lives. Stephen R. Covey asks us to look at the word *responsibility* as "response – ability." We are the master mechanics for the vehicle of our body, mind and spirit. We can choose to "respond" to the world with curiosity rather than boredom, with wonder rather than contempt, with respect rather than scorn and with joy rather than apathy. This requires that each of us become an "authentic" person, one that is willing to be honest about thoughts and feelings. We must then exercise, on a daily basis, high integrity choices based on love and confidence.

Integrity means communicating honestly while at the same time caring about the other person's feelings. Love refers to the self-love and self-respect you have earned by stepping through the door and onto the path of self-awareness. By communicating from the inside out you will begin to discover that growth is a cycle that involves an interaction between the outer and inner world. Each time you choose a positive response to the outer world, you alter the "reality" of your inner world. And each change takes you a step further on your journey toward self-discovery and actualization.

This collage uniquely expresses one person's self-concept. "The Nature of The Flower is To Bloom."
Alice Walker

Unit One: Beginning the Journey

The Journey of Growth Is a Journey That Creates Winners

An attitude that we must overcome is the challenge we often hear calling ou
from the depths of our consciousness that says "I dare you to make me grow!
Frederick Koenig echoes this idea, "We tend to forget that happiness doesn't com
as a result of getting something we don't have, but rather of recognizing and
appreciating what we do have." Many of us have lost faith in our ability to expand
beyond our current limitations and become reborn as our true selves. We see the
achievements of others and begin to feel like losers.

We want to stress that the journey of self-growth **is not** competitive. It is no
a win/lose model of human interaction that says only a certain percent of the
population gets to be wonderful, self-actualized, whole and healthy people while the
rest of us get to be stepping stones. Working toward self-awareness is a win/win
situation. A victory for one person opens the door for others to follow. And ever
step you take toward understanding yourself better enables you to communicate in
a healthier manner in all of your relationships. You then become a role-model fo
others to do the same. That's what is so wonderful about this process—we all ge
to be winners!

WHERE TO BEGIN

Finding the keys to the doors of greater self-esteem and awareness is great, a
long as you can also figure out how to use the keys. This book is a guide to tha
process. Adopting these constructive attitudes is the important first step. We asl
that you begin the journey by considering the following methods:

- Be open to new ideas and concepts. Assuming we already "know" everythin,
prevents us from being open to change.

- Study what is "inside" of yourself as well as what is "outside."

- Be open to learning from others. We are mirrors for each other's growth.

- Realize that in every situation you have alternatives to choose from. Thes
alternatives include choosing how to feel about yourself and others.

- Awaken your own interest in the subject of self-concept in the following ways

    Participate in discussions on the subject, read information, get to know
    people so you have some additional feedback, talk to experts (teachers
    counselors and the like), see yourself using the ideas in your life and
    finally, treat the subject as if it were "alive" and important to you.

homophobia

As we develop stronger, more centered self-understanding we become aware of more space in our lives to help others do the same. We are no longer expending time and personal energy on self-punishment. We are increasingly living each moment as happier, more productive human beings. It becomes part of our function to help others find peace and productivity as equally unique and worthy people. When we give ourselves the gift of self-esteem we become like open doors. Through our example others recognize they can begin to unravel the mysteries of self discovery for themselves.

As teachers, we recognize that we are all on this journey together. As inhabitants of this beautiful world, the more we increase our self-awareness, the more prepared we are to help each other as well as the planet. We do not view ourselves as the "experts." We are simply here to help you re-discover potentials within you. So, we begin this journey with these words from the book *The Dancing Wu Li Masters,*

"The Wu Li Master does not speak of gravity until the student stands in wonder at the flower petal falling to the ground. He does not speak of laws until the student, of his own, says, 'How strange! I drop two stones simultaneously, one heavy and one light, and *both* of them reach the earth at the same moment!' He does not speak of mathematics until the student says, 'There must be a way to express this more simply.' In this way, the Wu Li Master dances with his student. The Wu Li Master does not teach, but the student learns."

Chapter Two
DISCOVERING WHO WE ARE

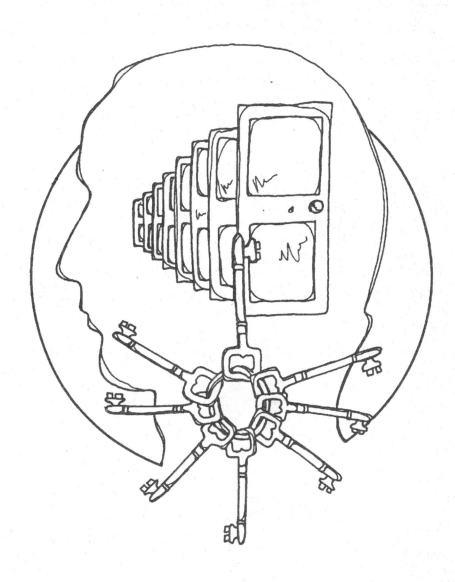

SELF-CONCEPT

We cannot hide who we are and ask strangers, hiding who they are, to love us and expect to find happiness.

Leo Buscaglia, *Born To Love*

Throughout the centuries philosophers, psychologists and educators have agreed with Socrates that the central core goal of mankind is to *"KNOW THYSELF."* This is easier said than done because we are rarely taught how to find ourselves, let alone know ourselves! The journey of self-discovery may seem long and difficult but must begin with the first step by answering the age old question "Who Am I?" This chapter's goal is to help you find out *who* you are, how you feel about yourself and why. We hope that because of your willingness to seek answers about your own path of self-discovery, you will find doors opening, beyond which lie riches waiting to be claimed.

THE FIRST STEP—UNDERSTANDING OUR SELF-CONCEPT

The self-concept is defined as "the relatively stable set of perceptions that a person holds about himself." These self-perceptions make up how we see ourselves and largely determine "what" we reveal to the people around us. In order to truly describe ourselves it would take hundreds of different aspects. One study alone identified approximately 18,000 words in the English language that can be used to describe aspects of our personalities.

For some people, this task of describing themselves is relatively easy. Those people are considered to possess a high state of *SELF-AWARENESS*. But for many others, the task of answering "WHO AM I?" proves to be difficult because they have not been taught to look inward. Wherever you find yourself right now is the starting point of your journey of self-discovery, because no matter how much you know about yourself, there is ever so much more to explore.

16

A better understanding of *ourselves* will also bring us closer to an understanding of *others*. When we are able to accept the often unpredictable ways in which we behave and think, we can begin to see more clearly why others act and react the way that **they** do. An old American Indian adage says that we can't understand anyone else until we have walked a mile in their moccasins. We recommend that we become more comfortable in our own moccasins before we try to fit into anyone else's.

WE SEE OURSELVES THROUGH OUR SELF-IMAGE

As you begin to explore your "self" you will become aware of your **SELF-IMAGE.** Your self-image includes how you view yourself as a person and how you view your appearance. An increased focus on self-image seems to be taking center stage in the current era, with more and more people seeking to model themselves after "beautiful people." Many studies point out that, because of the strong influence of the "beauty myth," which has been fostered by the mass media, our self-images have begun to take precedence over other areas of our self-concept, especially so with teenage girls and women. According to a 1990 survey by the American Association of University Women, regardless of the educational level, women do as well as men academically, yet their self-esteem drops dramatically over the years. Both sexes report that they are "happy the way I am" when they start grade school yet by high school it has dropped to 46 percent for boys and to a frightening low of 29 percent for girls!

What makes this trend even more frightening is that women are becoming the victims of "bad body images" at younger and younger ages. Rita Freedman, professor of psychology and women's studies reports in her book *Bodylove* on a round of studies that found a majority of ten year olds rated themselves as the single LEAST attractive girl in their school class; teenage girls said they frequently felt ugly; fewer than half of college women felt good about their appearance; a majority of adult women considered themselves heavier than they really were, as well as heavier than the ideal they thought men preferred, and women considered 'pretty' by others were just as likely to be dissatisfied with their looks as were women considered 'plain.'

Interestingly enough, men and women react to self-image differently. "Teenage girls' self-esteem is significantly lower than boys, probably because the girls abide by such 'punishing and paradoxical standards of attractiveness'," explains Susan Harter, Ph.D., a professor of psychology at The University of Denver who studies self-esteem across the life span. However, it appears that men are beginning to feel the effect of outside influences and are experiencing more dissatisfaction with their bodies as well. If an average is taken of many recent studies "70 to 90 percent of all males would now like to change something about their appearance, a third

Unit One: Beginning the Journey

would consider cosmetic surgery, and more than half don't like how they look naked." And this dissatisfaction seems to be starting very young. In a 1992 study at the University of Iowa over 450 fourth graders were surveyed about their body images. Sixty percent said they wished they were thinner, worried about being fat and weighed themselves **every** day. It is clear that our cultural emphasis on appearance and image leads people to believe they are "NOT ENOUGH!" Unfortunately, more of us need to adopt the attitude of writer Edna LeShan, "People are wonderful-looking. I love animated smiles and eyes that show feelings. Short or tall, fat or thin, bald or curly-haired, every person I have ever seen looks interesting to me....For every person who is beautiful there are several million of us who are not—and most of us are doing all right, thank you."

SELF-ESTEEM AND ITS INFLUENCE

In 1990 the California Task Force to Promote Self-Esteem and Personal and Social Responsibility, a 29 member panel of specially selected mental health professionals and educators, defined self-esteem as: "Appreciating my own worth and importance and having the character to be accountable for myself and to act responsibly toward others." There are many similar definitions, but generally self-esteem is like an internal barometer of contentment with one's self. Most experts agree that a person with high self-esteem has learned to feel good about himself because he likes what is on the inside and is not as concerned about material possessions or the impressions others have of him.

The greatest benefit from high self-esteem is that it enables us to live happier and healthier lives. Reports a study from the University of Michigan on well-being in America, "the best predictor of general life satisfaction was not satisfaction with family life, friendships, or income, but *satisfaction with self.*" It seems that people who possess high self-esteem focus their energies on enhancing their INNER awareness. And people who like and accept themselves feel good about life in general." As Ralph Waldo Emerson stated "Though we travel the world over to find the beautiful, we must carry it within us or we find it not."

enhance (v) to improve the quality, amount, or strength of sth

LOW VERSUS HIGH SELF-ESTEEM

As more and more people suffer the impact of negative self-images, more and more problems related to low self-esteem become apparent. The California Task Force's studies determined low self-esteem to be "the single most important factor underlying social ills such as academic failure, drug use and crime." A startling concept began to emerge in these studies—a greater emphasis on developing higher self-esteem in our nation's students can serve as a "social vaccine" against many

18

of the major social problems of the day. Wanda Urbanska in her article entitled "
Self-Esteem—The Hope of the Future" asks us to consider this: "Once introduced
into an individual's behavioral system (like a bacterial vaccine into the body), self-
esteem can help one live responsibly and ward off the lures of crime, violence,
substance abuse, teen pregnancy, child abuse, chronic welfare dependency, and
educational failure."

Self-esteem levels determine whether life puts you on a diet or provides you with a smorgasbord

Unit One: Beginning the Journey

phân biệt

At this point we want to draw a distinction between self-esteem and egotism Some individuals view high self-esteem as simply a "braggart" tooting their own horn! However, we believe that egotism is masked low self-esteem. Consider the following behaviors as identified by Adler and Town in *Looking Out, Looking In*. low self-esteem person disapproves of others, rejects others more easily, reacts t negative feedback, feels threatened by people he views as superior and is mor likely to evaluate his own performance negatively when compared to someone o high self-esteem. These are typical behaviors of a person who is relatively ego invested and not capable of being able to positively express self-esteem. I contrast, a high self-esteem person is more likely to think well of others, not b afraid of others' reactions, expect to be accepted by others as well as feel comfortabl around people that he views as superior and will evaluate his own performanc more positively than someone with low self-esteem. A high self-esteem person doe not need to brag in an effort to feel better about himself. On the contrary, if a hig self-esteem person brags, it is usually to share his accomplishments for the shee joy of sharing and encouraging others!

It is possible that you are caught up in a tide of self-destruction and do no believe in your own uniqueness nor love yourself enough to overcome obstacle and become a survivor of life. A recently divorced, forty-two year old studen expressed in class one day that she felt "worthless . . . not wanted by a man, company or friends who were busy with their own families." She had been feelin very depressed, spending a lot of time alone and painfully expressed that she wa not certain if it was worth it anymore. As she hesitantly revealed these feelings sh started to cry. Slowly, her classmates began to tell her what they liked about her At first, she would deny these positive attributes. Finally, the teacher told her t simply "listen" to what was being said and simply say "thank you" to eac student. She may have been sobbing by the end of class but later stated that tha moment was a turning point in her life. She suddenly wanted to turn he destructive thoughts around because she found one truth in what her classmate had said—she had **worth** as a person! It seems clear that self-esteem is so vital t healthy living that one can understand why self love has been recommended i most of the world's religion. As Leo Buscaglia, a writer dedicated to the facilitatio of self-esteem and love, states:

"Most religions of the world command that we love ourselves. The essence of the mandate is that we must be aware of the inherent harmony that exists between the love we feel for others and the love we must, of necessity, feel for ourselves, if we are to love at all. While some say otherwise, self-love is a healthy necessity and as long as it is directed outward, has nothing to do with egocentricity. Self-love is founded in the fundamental truth that we are only able to give what we have and teach what we know. The goal is to develop the best possible self, enabling us to share it with others. It is impossible to love others more than we do ourselves."

20

appraisal (n) the act of examining someone or sth in order to judge their qualities, success, or needs

influential (adj) having a lot of influence on someone or sth

linguist (n) someone who studies foreign languages or can speak them very well, or someone who teaches or study linguistic

REFLECTED APPRAISAL AND SOCIAL COMPARISON

imbecile (n) a person who behaves in an extremely stupid way

Now that you have a greater understanding of what self-concept is and how it is influenced by our self-image and self-esteem let us explore how it is formed. Most researchers agree that we are not born with a self-concept. Although science is beginning to determine that some personality traits may have a genetic (adj) di truyền component, a baby before the age of six months does not consider himself as being different (phân biệt) from his surroundings. By six months of age a child begins to distinguish himself from others in his life. His personality becomes more distinct (noticeable (adj) khác biệt) and he learns who are the significant people in his life. From that point forward the people that are important to him will be influential (adj) to his self-concept. What they say and how they say it will help him shape and evaluate his self-image and realize his worth. Psychologist Charles Cooley has called this process **REFLECTED APPRAISAL**. Reflected appraisal means that your self-concepts develop out of the "reflections" you receive about yourself from others. It's as if their view of who you are is **mirrored** back. This idea makes the presence of loving relationships in your life important, especially when you are young and take the comments of your significant family members to heart. Leo Buscaglia states "Psychologists and linguists tell us that before we are young adults it is likely that we will have heard such negative words as 'stupid,' 'idiot,' 'nuisance,' (phiền phức) 'imbecile,' (ngu) and 'obnoxious,' (đáng ghét) directed toward us over 15,000 times....It is no small wonder that many spend a lifetime dealing with feelings of inferiority." (n) someone is considered to be less important than other people. (by which way / method) whereby (adv)

Self-development is a lifelong process whereby we receive positive and negative feedback from our significant others about our importance, potential, capabilities (tiềm năng) (n) khả năng, and self-worth. Our self-concept is confirmed anew or challenged with each significant input we receive. Unfortunately, many of us who grew up in families or environments in which the negative inputs outnumbered the positives have come to this stage of our journey with damaged self-esteem. Results of studies taken on adults point out that the major component (n) cấu tạo thành phần in determining self-esteem levels is the presence of a positive and affirming parent. One of your author's brothers shared that his reoccurring problems in relationships could be traced back to when he was seven years old and his parents were getting a divorce. During the child custody (n) quyền nuôi con suit (n) legal problem his father told the judge that he wanted his daughter and his son could "go with his mother." The son felt this act reflected a negative appraisal by his father and he struggled with feeling worthy of a healthy relationship after that. How often have you received too much positive reflective appraisal from those you care about? If your answer is "rarely," then consider what messages you have received and how they have reflected on your self-esteem. The better the image we see in the mirrors around us, the better we will feel about ourselves.

The second important idea that can explain how our self-concept is formed is **SOCIAL COMPARISON**. Social comparison means evaluating yourself in terms of how well you compare to others in your important reference groups. Your reference groups includes your friends, classmates, fellow employees and so on. Do you find

• obnoxious (adj) very unpleasant or rude

• reference group — a group to which a person or another group is compared when you are studying the effects of sth.

Unit One: Beginning the Journey

yourself more or less attractive than your peer group or your friends? Do yc
see yourself as more or less popular? Intelligent? The impact of social comparisc
is quite evident to one of the authors. When she was growing up she never thougl
of herself as poor, because all of her relatives were generally poorer than h
immediate family. Thirty years later, her own children have a large number
reference groups ranging from television to classmates. In comparing themselv
to these groups they sometimes see themselves as "poor," "not as pretty," not a
"popular" and so on. It is true that the higher the standards of the group that v
compare ourselves to, the greater the difficulty for our self-concept and sel
esteem. It is easy to feel that we simply do not "measure up."

*"You can make more friends in two months by becoming interested in other people than you can in tu
years of trying to keep other people interested in you."*   Dale Carnegie

A very frustrating component of social comparison which adds to our increase
dissatisfaction with ourselves is the trend toward comparing our image to that c
the "perfect person" as shown to us in the media. We have already seen that th
unrealistic, ideal images of the mass media's "beauty myth" have had damagin
effects on our self-images and therefore our self-esteems. More than one generatio
has grown up comparing themselves to the few other people they perceive a
"perfect." It is unwise for you to even try to compete with this ideal. This kind c

impact (v) have an influence on sth

designate (v) to choose someone officially to do a particular job

affectionate (adj) showing feeling of liking or love.

comparison can lead to feelings of inferiority. Many students that we have found in our classes over the years set such unrealistic expectations for themselves that they repeatedly set themselves up for failure. They wish to be as pretty as their favorite model, as popular and famous as their favorite TV or movie star, and as smart as Einstein. These unrealistic expectations can only lead to a self-defeating cycle.

self-defeating (adj) used to describe sth that causes or makes worse the problem it was designed to void or solve

EDUCATION AND SELF-ESTEEM

The California Task Force on Self-Esteem determined that following the family, "school is the single most important factor in damaging or fostering self-esteem." The tremendous impact that teachers can have on the success of students has been demonstrated by Dr. Robert Rosenthal and Lenore Jacobson in their landmark studies *Pygmalion in the Classroom.* Children were identified at random as being students who would be "intellectual bloomers." The random list of intellectual bloomers was given to the teachers. In reality, the only difference between these children and their peers was "in the minds" of their teachers. At the end of the school year the teachers were asked to describe the classroom behavior of all their pupils. "The children in the group designated as the bloomers were seen as more interesting, more curious, and happier. The teachers also found the 'blooming' children slightly more appealing, better adjusted, and more affectionate, and with less need for social approval." Even more interesting, is that the average gain on an IQ test was found to be four points more than their counterparts, and seven points more on reasoning abilities. A side note that Rosenthal and Jacobson found was that "many of the other children in the classes also gained in IQ during the same year, but that the teachers had reacted more negatively to 'unexpected' improvement. The more the undesignated children gained in IQ points, the more they were regarded as LESS well adjusted, LESS interesting, and LESS affectionate."

Reflect back on your schooling and consider which of your teachers helped you facilitate a positive self-fulfilling prophecy about yourself, and which were more of a negative influence on your self-concept or self-esteem? Hopefully, the cumulative effects of the positive affirming teachers outweighed the negative for you. If not, the later discoveries on our path to mine our hidden talents will provide the tools to recreate your image more as you want it to be. Because your past programming has led to the creation of poor self-esteem, is no reason you have to stay stuck with it forever. This journey is about self-change and self-enhancement. We hope to help you seek out and cultivate the Positive Pygmalions of your life. And, most importantly, to **be** a positive pygmalion for yourself.

Unit One: Beginning the Journey

BRINGING POSITIVE PYGMALIONS INTO OUR LIVES

Whoever fulfills the role of a pygmalion for you and has an effect on your self-esteem can be influential in contributing to your *self-fulfilling prophecies.* Whether this person is a parent, teacher or friend, if he or she gives you reflected feedback often enough you may begin to believe you "are" what you are told you are. If you are told you are "stupid, slow and dull," you may develop a self-fulfilling prophecy by adopting those qualities because you believe them to be true. A student shared in class that she had a low self-esteem because her father had always told her that she wasn't as strong or smart as her brothers. It wasn't until she was involved with her boyfriend that this self-image began to change. Recognizing what her problem was, her boyfriend started telling her something positive about her physical condition or her intelligence at least once a day. She claims "I've been with him over a year now and I'm just beginning to believe that maybe I'm not so bad after all!" The influence of the self-fulfilling prophecy then points out the power of the pygmalions in our lives to help us change our outdated images. For example, Jack Canfield reports on a study that followed school kids around during a day measuring the positive and negative comments made to them. Unfortunately, there were approximately 4 negatives for every one positive comment made. For those of us who desire to become positive pygmalions with those around us, we need to reverse that ratio—four positives for every constructive criticism!

As we stated earlier, the journey begins with each of us answering the question Who Am I? How do I feel about myself? And how do I see myself? Some of us have a longer distance to go in repairing a damaged self-concept or self-esteem. But don't worry—wherever you find yourself you can always map your own exploration to greater self-acceptance and self-esteem. This book will describe a variety of paths that can be traveled towards your true self. Perhaps one or more of these paths will attract you, or you may reject them. The choice of whether you stay on the well-traveled path of your past or choose an adventure on the "road less traveled" to a greater self is up to you. Whatever road you choose, trust it. Listening to and following these internal signals is itself the beginning of the journey.   Leo Buscaglia says it best, "The human mind can imagine both how to break self-esteem and how to nurture it—and imagining anything is the first step toward creating it. Believing in a true self is what allows a true self to be born."

• self-fulfilling prophecy : a self-fulfilling prophecy is a prediction that directly or indirectly causes itself to become true, by the very terms of the prophecy itself, due to positive feedback between belief and behavior.

24

Chapter Three
PERCEIVING A NEW YOU

PERCEPTION

Reality! What a concept!!

Robin Williams

As we discussed in the previous chapter, we are treasure houses of intricate (adj) mysteries just waiting to be explored and understood. Our self-image and self concept are just part of a very complex process, that, if developed, can lead to greater self-awareness. To further understand that process it is now important to examine the role of perception, for it not only influences the way we form our self-concept, but also impacts the ability we have to change our past programming. After all, remember that the definition of the self concept is "the relatively stable set of **perceptions** that a person holds about himself."

The goal of this chapter is to explore the manner in which we form our perceptions. The perception process is intimately connected to how we process information. The more we understand about this process, the more we will maximize our abilities and improve the way we communicate both within ourselves and with others.

THE PERCEPTION PROCESS

Perception is defined as the process by which you sense, process, organize and interpret your **reality.** You see, feel, hear, taste and smell the world and then you assign meaning to that information. The way in which you translate this sensory data into meaningful pictures is called **information processing**. It is valuable to understand exactly what this amazing system is—and is not—capable of Philosopher Samuel Bois has stated that, "99% of W.I.G.O. ("What Is Going On"— outside our brains) cannot be processed by our information processing system. He refers to this limitless world as etcetera (ETC.) or the greater world that lies outside of the field of our awareness. Yet, at the same time, the amount of information you do process and interpret is impressive. You can gain a glimpse of the immensity of

neuroscientist (n) a scientist who studies the nervous system and the brain.

arouse (v) arousal (n): cause someone to have a particular feeling
└ feel sexual excitement

this "world" by looking at the complexity of your vision and hearing. David Mortensen, in his book *Communication: The Study of Human Interaction*, states that "the average eyes are capable of making up to 5 million visual discriminations per second and can differentiate up to 7 and one/half million different shades of color. Likewise, the ear is enormously sensitive, enabling a person with normal hearing to distinguish between 340,000 separate tones." It is clear to see that, despite some limitations, human perception is extremely acute. acute

However, despite the enormous capacity, the human information processing system is limited by how much physical energy it can monitor at any given point. You would go on "sensory overload" if you tried to perceive all the information that is constantly bombarding you (the sights, colors, sounds, smells, etc., that constantly compete for our attention.) You have a definite limit to the amount of information which you can identify at any given moment which is called your **channel capacity.** For example, you can generally recognize about seven items of information at one time. For more difficult material, you are capable of monitoring five different features simultaneously.(cùng một lúc)

○ Threshold (n) a point at which sth starts

THE FIRST STEPS TO PROCESSING INFORMATION

stimulate (v) to encourage something to grow, develop, or become active

Much of what is currently known about how the brain functions indicates that what you perceive is not *the real world*, but just a portion that you have selected to perceive. In order to cope with the overwhelming amount of sensory input you are exposed to, the normal brain appears to filter out a large portion of this information. This narrowing of focus is referred to as **selective perception**. Out of all the competing sensory data, you "select" what is important enough to pay attention to. This act of selective perception is necessary for you to simply cope with daily life.

The brain often perceives what is "important" by what sensory inputs are most powerful. Dr. Candace Pert, a neuroscientist with the National Institute of Mental Health, explains that you have an individual "arousal threshold," a point at which you are stimulated by the external world. If an outside stimulus is brighter, louder, larger than life, it has the greater chance of breaking your arousal threshold. For example, the normal attention span of people who consistently watch music videos is 15-45 seconds. Have you ever noticed all the movement and contrast between the images on these videos? This demonstrates how the brain responds to diversion, movement and change, and how the marketers of music videos understand what appeals to your selective perception.

The brain does not entirely ignore **repetitious** information. Sometimes you need information or an action to be repeated in order to learn or remember it. Repetition can help to embed messages into your awareness if they are restated 3 to 5 times. Any more often, and the brain becomes bored due to the lack of change or contrast.

○ consistently (adv) in a way that does not change
○ repetitious (adj) filled with unnecessary and boring things expressed or happening in the same way many times.
○ embed (v) to include text, sound, image ... on a computer file

27

nag (v) to criticize, or complain often in an annoying way

Unit One: Beginning the Journey

For example, if someone repeats a message too frequently, it leaves you feeling nagged.

The process by which you create your perceptions is very complex. Before you can interpret and react you must **organize** the input into a perceptual framework that serves you, as well as one that confirms your belief in the world. Perception must always be considered a combination of the incoming flood of information, the way it's being filtered and the manner in which it is organized into a meaningful pattern. Dr. Crick, a neuroscientist at the Salk Institute in LaJolla, California, says it this way, "The cortex (of the brain) is like a machine looking for correlations . . . millions of interconnected neurons chatter and babble to each other, the total of which combines for a unified perception that makes SENSE to us."

Your reaction to what you perceive depends on your **interpretation** of the incoming information. Your individual interpretation will depend on your unique past experiences and personal history. **No** two people perceive the **world** exactly alike. To expect another person to have exactly the same view of a situation as your own is not realistic—nor is it possible. There is always room for misunderstanding because of the natural process of "distortion" that occurs when data filters through your individual information processing system.

"If I were looking through your eyes I wonder what I'd see. . . . And would I remember you better if I could see what you see?

"Someone Else's Eyes" Up With People

Perceiving a New You

PERCEPTUAL FILTERS

The manner in which we organize and interpret information is based on an intricate combination of filters. These filters are comprised of physical, mental and emotional factors that literally sift incoming information. Every person has a unique set of filters that influence his or her view of the world.

Physical Filters

You are born with additional physical characteristics that influence the way you perceive. For example, humans perceive a limited range of sound and light in comparison to certain species. Yet, humans have certain senses that are more evolved. For example, if you were looking at a black and white photograph of a group of people, you could perceive their expressions, body positions, clothing and other specific details. A dog, however, cannot perceive two dimensional reality so it would sense the texture and smell of the photographic paper. You further filter information if your physical senses are limited in any way. A person with color-blindness would experience a rainbow after a storm, very differently from others. And obviously the absence of any one of your physical senses changes the way you process information through the remaining ones.

A second important physical filter is what Bois refers to as the brain's **reducing valve**. Once you have selected what to pay attention to, you mentally reduce the information to make it manageable. Your day-to-day survival obviously depends on this filtering process or you would surely be overwhelmed. In fact, certain mental disorders occur when the filtering process is not functioning. For example, schizophrenics often show abnormal sensory acuity which creates confusion because of unfiltered competing sensory input. The reducing valve is also the way the brain filters information through neurochemistry. Dr. Pert stresses that the chemistry of the brain is a crucial component of the filtering system. She summarizes the impact, "As raw information from the universe, from the outside world, percolates up to higher levels of consciousness, it gets filtered at several stages. You screen reality . . . Every creature has its own window on the universe . . . Everybody's version is different."

Cultural Filters

In addition to the physical factors, your culture plays a big role in determining how you filter information. Your culture includes not only the society you live in but also your family upbringing, gender, age, health, breadth of experience, values, needs and motives. It is therefore important to consider the "whole person" when trying to understand how someone perceives the world.

Unit One: Beginning the Journey

Let's look at two of these personal factors, culture and age, as examples. It is clear that every individual is shaped by the culture and sub-culture into which they are born. Your cultural backgrounds teach you different ways of living and of perceiving the world. Even attitudes about the very nature of communication vary from culture to culture. Western cultures may view extroversion as a desirable trait, while some Asian cultures view introversion as a sign of politeness and wisdom. These differing attitudes can certainly lead to difficulties and misperception when members of the two cultures meet and communicate.

Cultural differences in ideals, values, and beliefs can lead to misperception as well. The varied role of women in the world demonstrates how wide the differences can be. Women raised in Muslim or Arabic cultures may be taught from early on to hide their facial and physical features from everyone except their family members and their husband. American women, who are used to being more open and expressive, may view this action as being "subservient" rather than acknowledging it as a different cultural perception. Great need exists in the world today to have more understanding and acceptance for the diversity of perceptions of the many cultures, sub-cultures and religions that exist in a shrinking world community.

Equally evident should be the differences in perception created by the so-called "Generation Gap" which is based on the differences of age and accumulation of life's experiences. Currently, many of the people over 60 years of age share a perception about the role of money and security based on their experience of The Great Depression and World War II. They often feel a conflict with the attitudes about money expressed by the so-called Yuppie Baby-boomers who grew up in an economic boom. Many "boomers" were taught to seek the good life and to expect the material benefits of an upwardly-mobile lifestyle. Both of these generations contrast with the current generation who are growing into maturity at a time of diminished expectations and economic crisis. The solution to breaking down the generation gap is more understanding and communication between the generations.

polarity (n) (opposite) the quality of being opposite
∟ the quality in an object that produces opposite magnetic or electric charges

relay (v) : repeat sth u've heard, or to broadcast a signal, message, or programme or television or radio

Personality Filters

stimulation (n) an action / thing causes someone become more active/ enthusiastic / develop / operate

The role of personality may seem to be a less obvious factor in shaping your perception, yet it has a direct impact. There are many current theories *(lý thuyết)* about types of personalities. Some of the most informative studies of personality styles and the role they play in how you perceive external reality have been done by Carl Jung, Eysenck and Isabel Briggs-Myers. These personality factors identify sets of personality polarities. The most widely discussed set is that of extroversion versus introversion. Understanding where you fall in the range between extroversion and introversion will help you see how this filter influences your perception.

the opposite (sth) Contrary to public opinion, **introverts do not** lack social skills, but rather react based on a more sensitive gateway in the brain. This gateway is called the **Reticulating Activating System.** A great portion of sensory input never makes it through this gateway. Since the R.A.S. is more active in the brain of an introvert than in an extrovert, more sensory data is relayed to the brain for processing. Because of this greater amount of data flow, introverted personalities may feel overwhelmed by too much stimulation. *(kích thích in)* Therefore, the more introverted a person is, the more he must learn coping strategies for reducing inputs. This coping device is called "dampening down" which means to reduce the available external sensory stimulation to the brain by inhibiting behavior. The following are examples of this filter: *dampen (v) to make feelings (excitement / enjoyment) less strong.*

1. They observe the environment for clues much longer before they take action. They internally analyze their actions and the actions of others.

2. They tend to make fewer mistakes because of their increased self-analysis. *(n)*

3. They can concentrate their energies better on a task. They also work most effectively alone. *inhibited (adj) not confident enough to say or do what you want.*

4. They dislike making mistakes, and are more cautious about risk taking.

5. They like to have a certain space or territory *(n) area* that they can call their own. They resent invasion of that space. *invasion : xâm lấn, sự xông vào. to feel angry becus u've been force to accept someone / sth don't like (adj)*

6. They may be more inhibited in their use of facial expressions, gestures, and color or style of clothing. They do not like drawing unneeded attention to themselves and often feel self-conscious. They may have difficulty sustaining *(v) continue / maintain* direct eye contact with strangers.

7. When it's time to recharge their batteries, they prefer alone time. An introvert can find the chaos *(hỗn loạn)* at a loud party very draining. *(v) chảy ra (clear) ⟷ (adj) causing u to lose most of ur energy. very tired*

inhibit (v) prevent someone from doin' sth by making them feel nervous or embarrassed
∟ to slow down a process or the growth of sth

augment (v) increase the size or value of sth by adding sth to it.

stimulus (n) sth that causes growth or activity.

scenario (n)
kịch bản
- (possible event)
- a description of
possible actions
or events in the
future

≈ worst-case
scenario

spectrum (range)

a range of diff
positions,
opinions, etc
btw 2 extreme
points

gregarious (adj)
liking to be w/
other people.

An **extroverted** personality, because their gateway is more closed to incoming sensory data, has many of the reverse ways of adapting to the outer world. They learn to psychologically pump up or "augment" the environment, they take more risks and crave stimuli and attention. Their identifying features may be the following:

1. They crave interaction with other people. They like a breadth of friendships.

2. They like activity, surprise, and adventure. The worse case scenario (n) for an extrovert is BOREDOM.

3. Extroverts have a greater breadth of interests, but may not be able to concentrate for as long as an introvert. They do not work well alone.

4. Extroverts like to talk and are quite social. The further away from the middle of the spectrum, the more gregarious they are.

5. To recharge their batteries they will want to be with people. The more the merrier. They enjoy the stimulation of a loud party.

It is important to understand how these two personality factors create a filter for your perceptual processing. It is equally important to **not judge** where you are on the continuum. Remember, different cultures place different values on each characteristic. And these factors are just one part of a very intricate information processing system.

REALITY AS WE CHOOSE IT TO BE

In addition to physical, mental and emotional filters, there are numerous other factors involved in the processing of information that can lead to distortion and misperception. As we examine these limitations we will discover new keys for creating the most accurate perceptions for our travels along the road to self-renewal and self-creation.

"Seeing Is Believing"

Almost eighty percent of the brain is devoted to visual processing—most of this being at the subconscious level. We tend to have a great belief in what is immediate and obvious to our visual field. We think, if we can't trust our eyes, what can we trust? As Samuel Bois notes, "We have learned to believe it as the true picture of reality. When we think we see (as we say) with our own eyes, we are actually projecting upon the world the picture of it that we have unconsciously created in our brain as we learn to interpret the retinal image. Our belief in the reliability of this interpretation is stronger than any information that goes against it."

"Believing Is Seeing"

Because we tend to look for events that confirm our world view and belief systems, the reverse adage can also be true, **believing is seeing.** Sometimes we do not see what is actually there, but what we believe "should" be out there. Our assumptions and our experiences act as a psychological filter in our perception. For example, a former student told the story of how he had plans to meet his girlfriend at a party. Upon arriving he looked around and finally spotted her in a corner. She was standing very close to another man, laughing and whispering. The student became furious, stomped out and left her there. He felt very foolish the next day when she revealed that the other man was her cousin and, in fact, they were discussing the surprise party she was planning for him. Obviously, this student allowed the visual perception to guide his actions.

This attitude of "believing is seeing" is referred to as a "psychological set" or "expectancy." You have belief systems and values that create **sets** from which you **expect** the world to be a certain way. When you encounter someone with a different "set" and you do not acknowledge **her** right to view the world that way, you will experience conflict. It is important to become wiser in our "created reality" and realize how often we delude ourselves by ignoring what is in front of our eyes. William Blake warns us against assuming the validity of our senses in his poem,"

> *This life's five windows of the soul*
> *Distort the heavens from pole to pole*
> *And teach us to believe a lie*
> *When we see with, and not through, the eyes.*

Emotions and Perception

Other important elements that may determine our perception of the world are our bodily needs and emotions. For example, several studies have shown that feelings of hunger can cause us to have illusions about what we perceive. Sailors who have been deprived of food saw blurred drawings as a fork, knife, or a swirl as a juicy fried onion ring. Emotions also have an impact. Anyone who can remember the first blush of "LOVE" can attest to how often you think you see your beloved walking ahead of you. Sometimes, when we are "in the emotion of love" we fail to see many things that are in front of us. As they say, "love is blind."

A greater understanding of this part of the process can be explained by how the brain always presents you with a reduced image of reality which can be distorted by your own filtering process. This formed image of what is actually there is called a "gestalt." Stage hypnotists count on this "gestalt making" process when they impress you with their illusions. Unfortunately, our brains and senses can be fooled by more that just stage illusions. Have you ever made a first impression of a person, "he is such a snob," or "she is so sincere," and later found out you were **dead wrong.** Studies have shown that most people need only a 10 second glance of someone to form a "gestalt" of how they will act. Then, because of our "expectancies" about their behavior, we will treat them according to our image, not necessarily because of who they really are. It is sad but true that we cling to our first impressions even when wrong. Equally sad is that, unless we have learned otherwise, we tend to favor negative impressions of others over positive ones. These are called misperceptions.

PUTTING IT ALL TOGETHER

All of the filters and factors which shape your perception of "reality" can be called "attentional spotlights." They are like internal beams of light that allow you to perceive whatever you shine them on. Without the ability to use these spotlights, you may feel like you are stumbling in the dark. The more you filter information and let other perceptual factors "dim" the way you see reality, the narrower your spotlight becomes. Therefore it is important to know how to literally **enlarge** your beam to take in more information and to allow it to present a brightly colored lens on the world. We recommend the adoption of the following to help lighten the path to self-awareness:

Perception Checking

Perception checking allows you to "shed light" on situations and interactions to gain a greater understanding of them. It is done by:

1   Stepping back and gathering more information and data.

2. Looking at the situation from the other person's point of view.

3. Being empathic (walking a mile in someone else's shoes.)

4. Asking others for more feedback and clarification of their behavior before closing the book on your perception and taking a "foolish" action.

5. Checking what you have learned against your original perception.

If you think of the process of perception as putting a puzzle together, you know that the more puzzle pieces you place in the correct slots, the clearer the total picture will turn out to be. New pieces of data can help you to "reframe" your initial perceptions to more accurate ones. A good friend of one of the author's had been acting very "strange" recently. She was irritable, jumpy and acted angry towards everyone. Most of her friends very quickly learned to keep "a distance." The author decided to perception check and with a little patience, found out that the woman was being tested for breast cancer and was simply "scared stiff." She didn't know how to communicate her fear to others, so she resorted to anger instead. Without perception checking she might have gone through the situation alone, feeling more desperate every moment. Since science has demonstrated that we are each unique in our perception, no two individuals will ever perceive the exact same event, in exactly the same way. We can see how valuable it is to practice the above techniques of perception checking and to delay final perception as long as you can.

Pessimism Versus Optimism

Studies have shown that those who feel good about themselves tend to look for the good in others. If you carry an expectancy that the whole world is full of pain, negativity, and hurt you can create a **self-fulfilling prophecy** in which you "see, hear, taste, touch and feel what you expect to see, hear, taste, touch and feel." If you adopt an attitude of **pessimism** you will most likely expect the worst to happen. Pessimism has been found to be damaging not only to a person's self-esteem levels, but also to his health and well being. Research indicates that pessimists usually view the world through a dark lens, misinterpreting and screening out positive information. Pessimism has also been related to physically depressed states. One student who seemed to be pessimistic about life, commented when the teacher received a dozen roses as a thank you gift from another student, "how tacky, that there was a wilted rose in the bunch." The teacher was shocked that he would notice the one "negative" item, rather than the many positives. It is healthier for all concerned when you focus your attention on the "positives" that surround you.

A positive self-image produces an **optimistic** perception of life. A series of studies indicate that an attitude of optimism is a key element to handling stress, achieving success, and staying disease free. Charles S. Carver, professor of psychology at the University of Miami, found that an optimistic outlook—expecting a good outcome for the future—led to a more "successful rehabilitation in heart surgery patients, less post-partum depression in new mothers and a greater chance for sustained sobriety in recovering alcoholics." He found that optimists actively try to work through their problems, while pessimists tend to sweep them under the rug, which only makes things worse.

Unit One: Beginning the Journey

Closed-Mindedness versus Open-Mindedness

Too many people aim a narrow spotlight on what is around them and end up perceiving very little of what is going on. This perspective is called **tunnel vision**. Tunnel vision allows you to confirm **your** view of reality, but you do so by ignoring everything (opinions, information, experiences, etc.) outside of your limited view. When you do this, you reduce the field of "truth." You become very **closed minded** to any possibilities outside of your belief system. Abraham Maslow explained the results of this mind set, "If the only tool you have is a hammer, you will learn to treat everything like a nail."

The outcome of closed-mindedness is that you often alienate other people unless they support your perception of the world. One student was trying desperately to negotiate with his father who had a very narrow view of his son's future. The father could only see his son as an engineer and yet the young man did not feel he would be happy in that field. The level of closed-mindedness on the father's part was creating a great conflict in the relationship, so much so that the son felt he could no longer discuss any subject with him. There was no light shining between them at all.

Open-mindedness results from the willingness to overcome perceptual barriers and from the desire to gain a larger view of the world. Zen Master, Suzuki Roshi, recommended that you can accomplish this with the **beginner's mind.** "In the beginner's mind there are many possibilities, but in the experts, there are few."

The only limits to growth are the **limits** you **believe** to be possible. Approaching your life as a beginner, ready to accept and to learn will allow you to widen the beam of your spotlight. This is done by:

1. Believing in the "impossible." Reality is what you make of it.

2. Approaching the world with the openness of a child. Creative genius often comes from being open to "seeing" something in a new, fresh way.

36

3. Being open to suggestions and different points of view. In 1878 Western Union made the mistake of turning down the rights to the telephone because they did not see a use for an "electronic toy." Don't miss opportunities in your own life!

These mental attitudes can light the path to self-awareness. While it is true that you were born with certain personality traits—that your brain naturally filters information and that you have many deeply-rooted cultural perceptions—the choice is still yours to be **open** to new growth. By opening your mind to new experiences you can wash away old thinking patterns. Brain specialist Dr. Merzenich states "Your genes don't predestine you to be a surfer, a dreamer, a world-class chess player, a Mercedes mechanic, a Follies Bergeres girl, a drill-bit salesman or Jean-Paul Satre. Your accumulated thoughts and actions weave your neurons into the unique tapestry of your mind." The question is, what will you do with it? You are the explorer and the tools are here to help you decide.

Chapter Four
THE NEW FRONTIER

THE UNIVERSE OF THE BRAIN

As long as the brain is a mystery,

the universe will also be a mystery.

Santiago Ramon y Cajal

As we cultivate our self-awareness it is important to realize that this is best done by gaining an understanding of both the mental and emotional factors that influence our daily behavior. Our mental, emotional and physical potential is stored in what can best be called the "keeper of the keys" or what Dr. James Watson, co-discoverer of DNA, calls "the last and greatest biological frontier." This frontier, ready for our exploration, is the human brain. We store everything we believe about who we are—and what we are worth—within this small amount of space no larger than the size of our fist.

We invite you to begin a journey of self-discovery into this last great frontier—the brain. In 1989 President Bush and the U.S. Congress declared the 90's the DECADE OF THE BRAIN. With the advent of new brain technologies such as Magnetic Resonance Imaging (MRI) and Positron Electron Tomography (PET) more has been learned about the brain and how it works than has ever been known before. Research is focusing on how the brain works, how we can better teach creative thinking and how our educational system can help students achieve their full intellectual potential.

The purpose of this chapter is to explore the impact our understanding of the brain can have on our communication behavior. Here we may find keys to open th doors to growth. Just as the forty-niners came to the West prospecting for gold, there is much buried treasure in each of us waiting to be mined!

THE HUMAN BIOCOMPUTER

Peter Russell, in his book *The Brain Book*, talks about the incredible complexity of the brain, "It is amazing to consider that the whole of the world's telephone system is equivalent in connections to only one gram of your brain—a piece the size of a pea." For our purposes the brain can be simplified by thinking of it as a sophisticated computer, a "biocomputer." After all, the brain was the original working model for the inception of computer technology in the 1940's. Russell states "unlike an electronic computer, the brain can carry on a thousand different functions simultaneously, continually cross-referencing and integrating new information." Its complexity far surpasses modern technology. In order to create a computer that can do everything that the human brain innately does, it would fill Carnegie Hall, and yet could not conceive of a "NEW THOUGHT" if it was not programmed into it. Truly this three pounds of gray matter is quite miraculous!

At a practical level, just as with a computer, "inputs determine the outputs." In relation to the physical world this means "garbage in equals garbage out." How do these inputs combine to produce your self-image? Millions of inputs combine together depending on your unique life experiences, levels of education, work experience and cultural backgrounds to determine who you are today. Statements that you receive from parents, teachers, friends, peers, mass media and other sources are *input* in such an individual way as to evoke a core set of feelings about your self-image and self-worth.

The impact of these "inputs" can be further seen when you realize that, at any given moment, you are susceptible to "master programmers," those whose inputs you accept as most valid and who are influential in shaping who you are. For example, from birth to about five years old, parents or parental figures are the ones who fill that role. From 5 through 8 years old the master programming comes from your teachers, particularly in the specific area of what kind of a student you "think" you are. Soon after eight years of age the power of peer group influence begins to dominate you until peer pressure reaches its zenith in high school. How much you accept peer group approval will determine how quickly the so-called "age of reason" occurs, where you detach from the need for approval from others and become your own "master programmer."

IMPRESS YOUR FRIENDS! STAGGER YOUR COLLEAGUES!
HERE'S 20 TERRIFIC BRAIN FACTS TO SPRUCE UP YOR
NEXT CONVERSATION!

1. **Size** - Like a grapefruit

2. **Weight** - Like a head of cabbage.

3. **Gas Guzzler** - The human brain needs 20% of all blood pumped by the heart.

4. **Jane Fonda Meets Albert Einstein** - The human brain burns up as much sugar during prolonged mental work as your muscles do during prolonged exercise.

5. **That's J-e-l-l-o!** - Looks and feels like a mound of firm, opaque jelly that's just been turned out of a gelatin mold.

6. **Easily Handles Four for Bridge** - The human brain is covered by a grey matter that would be nearly large enough to cover a card table if it were possible to unfold it.

7. **Fruits & Nuts, So To Speak** - The brain's core contains islands or clusters of nerve cells that vary in size and shape from that of an almond to that of a plum.

8. **If You Had a Nickel For Every One** - The human brain is made up of some 100 billion nerve cells and 200 supportant cells.

9. **What Hippocrates Said** - "The brain is the most powerful organ of the body."

10. **Size Doesn't Count** - The human brain is smaller than that of porpoises, whales and elephants.

11. **Size Does Count** - The human brain is four times the size of a gorilla's brain.

12. **Reputation** - The most comple structure in the known universe

13. **Weighty Subjects** - The average man's brain weighs 1,349 g., while a woman's weighs 1,206 g.

14. **It Takes a Big Brain to Think Up Those Tiny Little Lilliputians** - Jonathan's Swift's brain weighed 2,000 g.

15. **The Final Word on Size** - One of the largest brains ever measured belonged to an idiot.

16. **Head Start** - When an embryo is only 23 days old, the brain has already begun to develop.

17. **Did He File for Major Medical?** In 1879, Sir William Macewen pioneered successful brain surgery.

18. **More Talk of Vegetables** - The brain stem has a shape and size somewhat like that of a large plant or vegetable.

19. **The Little Dictator** - The human brain controls all bodily activities.

20. **One Scoop or Two?** - Priest in ancient Egypt removed human brains when preparing mummies.

WE ARE WHAT WE THINK

As you learn more about how the brain functions, you discover the tools for becoming your own master programmers. As you put these tools to use, you become much more able to "re-program" your thoughts and feelings in a way that leads to a more positive self-concept and self-image. This process begins by understanding that each thought you process has a powerful psychological and physical effect. Let's look at this thinking process. The brain is made up of roughly 12 billion brain cells with trillions of possible connections to the body's nervous system. The processing of thoughts and images triggers the release of chemicals throughout the body. These chemicals evoke emotions and behaviors. Your brain, then, is referred to as an "electro-chemical interactive feedback system," which means that the "energy" of your brain chemistry produces a complex and constantly changing series of perceptions and actions.

Most inputs can be categorized as one of three main types: *Auditory inputs* (thinking and hearing words) *visual inputs* (images or pictures you have inside your head whether you create them, remember them or are influenced by outside sources) and *kinesthetic inputs* (physical sensations and movement of your body.) We are going to focus on auditory and visual inputs and their impact on self-awareness in this chapter. Kinesthetic inputs will be discussed later in a following chapter.

Auditory Inputs

This type of thought relates to self-concept in relationship to what you think, hear and say about yourself. Marshall Thurber and many general semanticists say that "at one level language creates everything about us, therefore it is imperative that we always speak with good intent." Buckminster Fuller, one of the foremost philosophers of our time, literally stopped all talking for a year for he felt it was negatively affecting his consciousness about who he was. Fuller, no doubt, would have agreed with the saying "we become what we say we are." Physicists, who have studied electrical activity in the brain, quantify the power of the auditory inputs in the following manner:

1. a random thought equals x (x = a unit of neuronal energy)

2. a thought about oneself created by oneself generates 10 to 100 times more neuronal energy of the brain than a random thought.

3. a thought about oneself that you hear from others is equal in energy to your own thoughts so it is 10 to 100 times greater than a random thought.

4. a thought about oneself spoken out loud is 100 to 1000 times greater in its neuronal energy and impact on our self-concept than a random thought.

Unit One: Beginning the Journey

Let's look at this process. Random thoughts require little energy because your personal investment and interest in them is usually small. Your energy output begins to grow when your thoughts evolve around your "self." Thoughts that exist at lower levels of energy output are those that involve issues that are not very important to you, such as "my hair is messy and I hope that I don't see my boyfriend looking like this." However, if your self-esteem is low and you start stewing about being too tall or not as successful as someone else, the amount of energy you are investing in those thoughts begins to increase. A thought about **you** that you hear from someone else can increase the energy involvement. What raises or lowers the energy at this point is determined by the source of the comment, the positive or negative nature of the content, and how much credibility **you give** the input when thinking about it. It is no doubt true, that if a stranger in a grocery store calls you a name or tries to ridicule you, you might not accept the input unless you already believe that what he says is true about you. If a significant person ridiculed you it would probably matter much more. Therefore, you can see that the degree that someone can hurt you is determined by your willingness to accept and give energy to the "thought."

The power of an auditory input grows when you say something out loud because speaking out loud is one of the most energy evoking actions that the brain is capable of. You must become aware of the impact of the words that you use when describing yourself. Is your self-talk nurturing you or destroying you? When you examine what impact words have on your electro-chemical system you can begin to see how you might *reprogram* your self-image more positively. If talking out loud about yourself produces 100 times more energy in the brain, you can clearly see why you should never be negative about yourself **out loud**. Thinking critically about oneself is one thing, but giving voice to such criticism can be very destructive. For example, we have all experienced being around an attractive woman who feels driven to belittle her own looks. We may suspect that she wants compliments or that she believes she has to downplay her physical beauty in order to have friends. What she doesn't realize is, that in order to negate the programming impact of what she says about herself, she needs to get approximately 100 compliments about her looks from others. This is a self destructive cycle that many people are caught in. If you watch people use negative self-talk for several weeks you may be sure that they become what their own words have been programming into their brains. Remember, in the biocomputer "garbage in equals garbage out"- especially so when it is **spoken**.

Luckily, we have found that the reverse is equally true. When you verbalize one positive statement, you can negate 100 old negative inputs! That is the beauty of becoming a purposeful master programmer. Let us return momentarily to the computer model. What do you do with an out-of-date program? You update the old with something more desirable. Just as you focus all of the energy of your auditory inputs towards new desired self-images, you can literally re-program outdated behavior that you no longer want or need. The physical body presents us with a good example of this. Dr. Deepak Chopra states in his book *Quantum Healing*, "If you could see your body as it really is, you would never see it the same way twice. Ninety-eight per cent of the atoms in your body were not there a year ago. The skeleton that seems so solid was not there three months ago. The skin is new every month. You have a new stomach lining every four days, with the actual surface cells that contact food being renewed every five minutes. The cells in the liver turn over very slowly, but new atoms still flow through them, like water in a river course, making a new liver every six weeks. Even within the brain, whose cells are not replaced once they die, the content of carbon, nitrogen, oxygen, and so on is totally different today from a year ago. It is as if you lived in a building whose bricks were systematically taken out and replaced every year. If you keep the same blueprint, then it will still look like the same building." As a rule approximately 10 ten percent of the cellular structure of the body is changed every 3 weeks and 25 percent by approximately six weeks. Therefore, most mental habits or counterproductive programming can be altered in this time frame.

Like the body, if you purposefully alter the blueprint—your thoughts about yourself—you can change your behavior. If you change your thoughts to positive goals and self-talk, it seems clear that billions of new cells will be responding to the new thoughts rather than repeating the old ones. If you persist in using negative self-images and concepts, you do so at your own peril and remain a victim of past programming. You become like a broken record. Again, the choice is yours.

VISUAL PROCESSING

Just as you can change your words to help change the "self-concept program" in your biocomputer, you can also change the pictures that are a part of your self-image. Exploring your visual processing will lead you to discover that the **PICTURES** you see of yourself and of your world can be more important than your words in determining the blueprint of who you are! We can appreciate the importance of visual thoughts by understanding how much of the brain is involved in processing them. Machines that monitor brain activity help illustrate that visual processing uses a large portion of the occipital lobes towards the back of the cerebral cortex, whereas a verbal thought tends to localize in the left hemisphere, in a space about the size of a quarter. Because the neuronal connections involved in a visual thought are many times more numerous than those involved with a verbal thought, we believe that their behavorial impact is more powerful.

The sayings **"A PICTURE IS WORTH A THOUSAND WORDS, or "SEEING IS BELIEVING"** take on new meaning when we consider the impact of visual thought. Therefore it benefits us to be very careful of the visual images we hold of ourselves.

co-ordinate (v) (combine) to make many different things work effectively as a whole.

Unit One: Beginning the Journey

If we are serious about changing ourselves for the better then we need to coordinate our self-talk with these powerful self-images. For example, one of the reasons that people who diet usually gain much of the weight back is that they fail to change the internal pictures of themselves as they change their eating habits. Consider the way you usually picture yourself. Does this picture reflect a negative self-image, an image you would like to change? If so, change truly becomes a product of the inner images you hold of yourself.

The use of "constructed visual thinking" has become quite popular in the last decade because of its effectiveness in creating change and outstanding performance. Commonly referred to as imagery or visualization it has found widespread use in athletics, the arts, business, education and medicine. Our intent is to focus on how you can create desired self-changes by more actively using visual thinking.

Using Visual Inputs

For example, how many times can you remember waking from a dream especially a nightmare, with your heart wildly beating and drenched with perspiration. Perhaps you were racing away from a man with a knife and for a moment after waking, you could even still see the man. This demonstrates that your nervous systems do not know the difference between a vividly imagined internal event and an external "real" event. If a mental picture in a dream can cause such a powerful physical reaction, it should be possible to purposefully use visual thinking in a controlled manner to gain positive changes. People who study visualization and imagery have found that they can enhance their performance in any sport, dance, or mental activity by practicing the desired *ideal performance* in the "mind's eye" prior to the event. . . . A study at the University of Ohio used visualization with amazing results. Ten top basketball players were divided into two teams of equal ability. One team warmed-up by shooting ten foul shots. The other team sat with their eyes closed and imagined themselves throwing ten perfect foul shots. The two teams then competed and the group that had visualized the shots outscored the team that had physically warmed up. In Los Angeles, a high school football coach hired a hypnotist to help his football squad learn to visualize. The most dramatic results occurred with the place kicker who was discouraged that he had missed his last five field goals. He practiced imaging successful field goals five minutes a day and before each kick.   He became a believer in creative visualization when he went on to kick 32 successful field goals in a row! *(m)*

As more and more research has demonstrated the ability of internal imagery and visualization to affect the body, more and more professional athletes are becoming adept at communicating to their body through imagery. In the past two Olympics most of our successful athletes have included visualization along with their physical training to prepare themselves for competition.   They visualize themselves successfully lifting weights, going over the high jump and racing the

enhance (v) to improve the quality, amount, or strength of sth

phenomenal (adj) extremely successful or special, esp in a surprising way

advance (v) (move forward) to go or move sth forward, or to develop or

spontaneous (adj) happenin' or done in a natural, often sudden way, wi'out any plannin'
or wi'out being force. *improve sth*

100 meters. As sports psychologist, Shane Murphy, director of sports science for the U.S. Olympic team, noted in U.S. News and World Report, August. 1992, "At the level of the Olympics nowadays, there's not a whole lot of difference among the athletes in terms of physical talent and training. Ultimately, it's going to come down to what's between their ears." *Finally, after a series of things have happened*

The new focus on the mental edge has become more widespread in everyday life. As Brad Hatfield reports in the US News and World Report, "The implications go way beyond sports. Whether it's an airline pilot, musician, surgeon, or CEO, everyone's goal is achieving peak performance." And all of this is through the enhanced use of the brain's capacities, especially mental imagery. There are many examples of the phenomenal impact of "what you see is what you get." While recovering from a motorcycle accident which had left him partially paralyzed, a 26 year old man read about the impact of visualization on behavior. Two weeks after his accident—while lying in the hospital in traction—he decided to learn to type in his mind so that when he got out of the hospital he would be able to earn a living. Every day he read a typing manual and then practiced typing in his mind's eye. Two months later he was through rehabilitation and was taken to a "real" typewriter. Guess how fast he typed? 80 words per minute! Most of us would be happy with that speed. More surprising, he had no errors because, while he was seeing himself typing in the "mind's eye," he did not imagine any mistakes.

Understanding the impact that your thoughts, beliefs and images have on your health has advanced so far that a new branch of medicine is emerging called "psycho-neuroimmunology" or PNI. The more that scientists can study the brain, the more proof there is that our thoughts and images affect our health. A best-seller in this field is *Quantum Healing* by Dr. Deepak Chopra. In it he gives many very compelling case histories of patients who "saw" themselves well and experienced "spontaneous remissions." As Dr. Irving Oyle, author of *The Healing Mind* states "It is possible to reprogram the computer (of the brain) by means of the conscious image of the healthy state. Combining visualization techniques along with current medical therapies has been found to be especially effective in turning the survival rate of childhood leukemia around from 79% terminal before the 1960s, to almost 72% survival rate in the 1990s. It appears that visualization techniques work even better with children. Scientists are not clear yet whether it is merely their commitment to their mental imaging or the content of the visualizations themselves. Most Doctors do not care—they just know it works and so are using visual processing techniques more and more.

TWO VIEWS FROM THE SAME MIND

Fortunately for the student of today, research on the brain is finding practical applications in the classroom. Linda Williams states in her book *Teaching For the Two-Sided Mind*, "In the last fifteen years research on the brain has exploded as

multitude (n) a large number of people or things

Unit One: Beginning the Journey

new techniques allow scientists to probe areas previously restricted to the realm o speculation. No research has stimulated more interest than that on the two halve of the brain, for in revealing that the hemispheres function differently, it suggest: that we can expand our concept of the intellectual processes." Split brain researcl began in the early 1960s. when, led by Nobel Prize winner Dr. Roger Sperry, a tean of surgeons at the California Institute of Technology attempted the firs commissurotomy on a man suffering with epilepsy. A commissurotomy is a radica operation that involves cutting of the corpus callosum which is made up of 200 t 250 million nerve fibers that connect the left and right cerebral hemispheres of th brain. Sperry's tests of this and other split brain patients soon revealed two **different** brains in the same body, both perceiving the world around them totall **differently** and, because of the severed corpus collosum, with **no communicatio** between them. In hundreds of tests on the split-brain patients, these doctor documented a strange *doubling* of the stream of consciousness. "The surgicall separated hemispheres of animals and men have been shown to perceive, lear and remember independently, each hemisphere evidently cut off from the consciou experiences of the other." Scientists began to refer to the two halves of the brai as if they were two distinct personalities. For example, the first patient, Mr. W. would go for his wife's throat with his left hand (controlled by the right hemispher when he was angry and save her with his right hand. Another lady would unbutto her blouse with her left hand and button it back up with her right hand. As a resu of the research on split-brain patients over the past 30 years we know a great de about the different processing styles of the two hemispheres.

Let us turn to the fascinating findings of "split-brain" research. The le hemisphere of the brain controls the right side of the body and appears to be th dominant hemisphere in about 93% of Americans. The left hemisphere seems t process stimuli in a **linear-sequential manner.** In other words, it takes incomin information and handles it in an orderly, step by step fashion. The left brain is th dominant brain in areas such as spelling, reading, writing and math and process almost 97% of all our speech. Therefore, it is commonly referred to as the **VERBA** brain and is clearly the hemisphere that handles our auditory inputs.

In comparison, the right hemisphere possesses the language level of a five-ye old and the vocabulary of a twelve-year old. It appears to be best at synthesizin innumerable facts, dates and images, detecting the "big picture," rather than ju the individual facts and can process a variety of information approximately 85 times faster than the left brain. It processes most of the visual and spati information from inside and outside of the body. Imagery, dreams, daydreams an visualization are handled by the right hemisphere. Nonverbal body cues and fac recognition are also processed here, whereas the labels and names are processed the left brain. Therefore, the right hemisphere may be thought of as the **VISUA** brain. It is also predominant in athletics, dance and body movement because of th multitude of inputs necessary for coordinated physical performance. While studyin expert marksmen, Brad Hatfield of the University of Maryland found that, rig

48

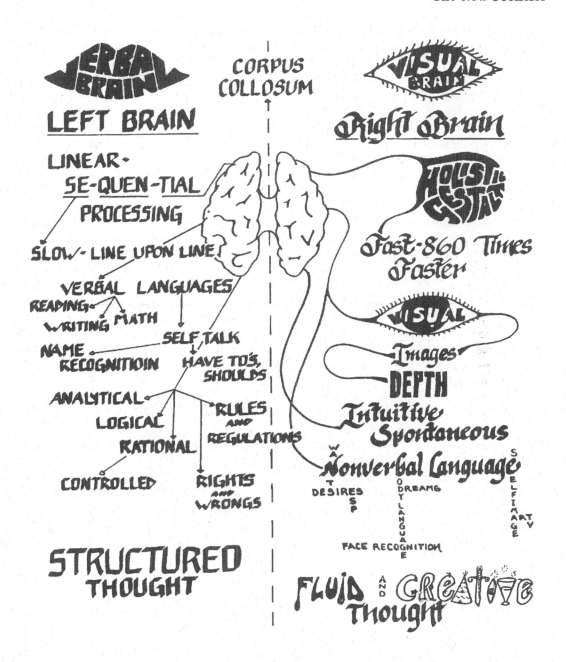

Figure #14–Split Brain

Unit One: Beginning the Journey

before shooting there was a shift from the left to the right hemisphere. He found that the mind relaxes its analytical left brain indicated by a sustained slow Alpha brain rhythm. The right brain then controls the body movements. "The result is a trance-like FLOW state that many athletes, musicians and other performers report experiencing when they are intensely engaged in an activity" states Hatfield.

Another major difference in the processing styles of the two hemispheres is that the left hemisphere processes anything which is determined to be logical, analytical, objective, causal, true-false or right-wrong within the cultural norms. Whereas the right hemisphere processes much of the information that is of an emotional, creative, impulsive and intuitive nature. Figure 14 demonstrates these and other major differences between the left and right hemispheres. Many researchers have speculated as to how and why the two hemispheres became so specialized. Most concur with Peter Russell in his book *The Brain Book,* "The value of specialization of function is that it effectively increases our mental capacity. Each hemisphere tends to analyze its own input first, only swapping information with the other side once a considerable degree of processing has already taken place. Thus we can process two streams of information at once and then compare and integrate them in order to obtain a broader and more sophisticated impression. Specialization of function also divides the load of each hemisphere. It is a very natural course of action to take for increased efficiency." Nature has given us two brains for the price of one and the question is how do we take advantage of them?

The tragedy is that our culture and the first twelve years of our educational system has fostered an over-reliance on the use of the left hemisphere's analytical style. We focus on reading, writing and arithmetic. It has become increasingly clear to educators that the synergistic, intuitive and creative functions housed in the right hemisphere, need greater facilitation if we are to access more of the potential we are born with. Enhanced creativity is a definite gift of the right brain processing style. For example, according to *The Brain Book*, Albert Einstein's greatest thoughts and ideas came through first as visualizations, pictures and diagrams. He said it was a great struggle for him to express these images in language. There is some speculation that he came up with the Theory of Relativity because he was able to think outside the structure of language. In the last decade some schools have been increasing the portion of the curriculum devoted to art, music and creativity with encouraging results. For example, at the Mead School in Bryam, Connecticut, the students spend half their time in art classes of one form or another and the other half in "regular" subjects. As a result, their performance in math, science, and a variety of other subjects has increased. It is also clear that most of the high scorers on SAT tests are those individuals who have learned by hook or crook to access the talent of both sides of the brain's hemispheres. Because of our cultural preference for the linear left brain, most of us are uneducated in the utilization of the more simultaneous and holistic style of our non-dominant right hemisphere. This is very unfortunate because most creativity, intuition, art, music and genius emerges from combining the best aspects of **both** styles of processing.

50

EXPLORING A NEW TERRITORY

As more and more brain research focuses on the processing styles of the two hemispheres, more and more emphasis is being placed on developing and teaching "whole-brain" or "connected thinking." Whole-brain or connected thinking simply means the ability to quickly switch to the hemisphere of the brain which can best serve your current need. For example, when you are dancing it is important to be able to shift into the "flow" state of the right hemisphere. If you stay in your left, analytical brain you will dance with "two left feet." If you stay in the less time-oriented "flow" style of the right brain while you are taking a history final, you will not remember enough of the facts to succeed on the test. Learning to gain quick access to both hemispheres is a vital key to unlocking the great potentials you are capable of.

How can you cultivate more "whole-brain, connected thinking" skills? First, you need to become aware of which hemisphere you tend to operate in. Are you very logical and good at English, math and history? Or do you favor creative activities such as art, athletics or music? Since we tend to prefer the "path of least resistance" we will gravitate toward classes and experiences that come more "naturally." Even though this allows you to develop your special talents, it can limit your experiences. So, first comes self-analysis and, once you know what your dominant processing style is, then comes practice. You merely have to choose experiences that allow you to use the neglected hemisphere. For one of your authors, the neglected hemisphere was the right one. She did not consider herself artistic, creative, athletic and felt that she lacked spontaneity. However, she received praise for her writing and speaking abilities and was rewarded with good grades for her logical and analytical style. It was easier to take subjects that she was "good" at. Although this

Rocky, an ambidextrous artist, demonstrates the relationship of the two hemispheres. When he uses his right hand his art becomes linear and structured, yet with his left hand it is fluid and formless.

helped her GPA, it shortchanged her development in more creative areas and caused stress whenever she encountered areas she was "not good at."

Unit One: Beginning the Journey

Whatever hemisphere you find yourself dominant in, the time has come to exercise your neglected one. Without the influence of outside forces, such as the educational system, the flow of brain dominance naturally moves every 90 minutes. If you are left brain dominant it is time to stop the critical, analytical inner voice and enjoy a creative activity. Who cares if you sing "off-key" or use the "wrong" color. It is time to get out of the way and utilize the aspects of both brains.

We will explain various ways to make greater use of your brain in later chapters but it's important to note now that you can externally stimulate and access the power of both hemispheres. An easy way to experience this whole-brain state is to listen to music because research has shown that music is the one single input which generally integrates the two hemispheres of the brain in a simultaneous fashion. Since music is a complex stimulus, the words, mathematics, beat and rhythm are processed by the left hemisphere while the right is processing the pitch, harmony, creativity and lyrics of the music. You can also utilize your whole-brain by becoming fluent in the "languages" of the two hemispheres which allows you to use more than the standard 10% of your brain potential. This conscious use of connected thinking is at the core of any creative whole-brain experiences such as art, science, athletics and dance and allows for greater retention and flexibility of thought. Research has shown that flexible thinkers are wrong fewer times than are left-brained thinkers. A much needed quality for the next decade is the increased flexibility of logical and creative thinking so that you might adjust to the constant change that you will be coping with. Some people may believe that you need bigger and brighter brains to deal with all the information we will encounter in the next few decades. We the authors disagree and feel that the brain is already BIG enough—we just need to learn **how** to use it. Dr. Marion Diamond, professor of Integrative Biology at U.C. Berkley, urges all of us, "It's not enough to sit and watch TV. Learn to challenge the brain—be involved!" Like most other parts of the body, the brain operates on the basic concept of **use it or lose it!** We are convinced that as you mine the buried gold of your brain, you will discover unlimited abilities. Those discoveries will change the very fabric of your self-image.

UNIT TWO
Further Explorations

Chapter Five
SELF-TALK AS
A KEY TO CHANGE

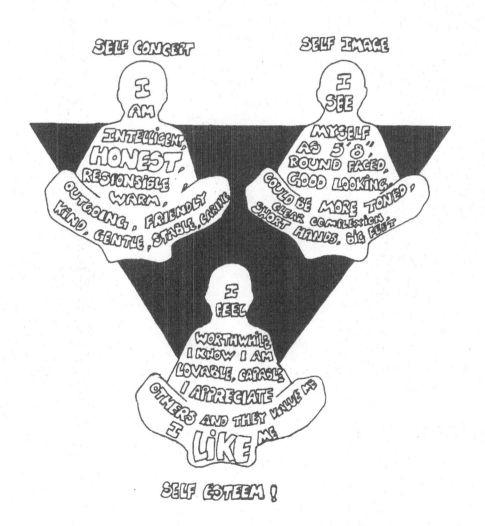

INTRAPERSONAL SEMANTICS

Words, like angels, are powers which have invisible power over us. They are personal presences which have whole mythologies....; and their own guarding, blaspheming, creating and annihilating effects.

James Hillman

Perhaps one of the most frustrating steps to take in developing a more positiv self-concept is taking control of the "inner voice." *Self-talk* refers to the interna dialogue we constantly have going on inside ourselves. Self-talk can be positive such as when we tell ourselves "I did that well!" or "Yeah, I look **good** today!" o it can be negative such as when we nag, whine, curse or put ourselves down. A we learned in chapter two, the quality and quantity of our auditory inputs, our sel talk, can have a tremendous effect on how we think, feel and act. The purpose c this chapter is to teach you how to exercise control over that "little" voice!

We will discover that through the use of semantic realignment and vocalize affirmations, you can learn the tremendous power of positive self-talk, which i turn will help you raise your self-concept, self-image and self-esteem. It i important that you understand that this is a tool for rewiring the brain an reframing any old outdated self-concepts that you no longer desire to maintair Many of these tools will help you in reshaping your future self.

CHANGING OUR SELF-TALK

One of the first steps towards changing our outdated internal programs is th conscientious use of *semantic realignment.* Semantic realignment means eliminatir the destructive words we use to describe ourselves and replacing them wit positive, energizing words. If we realize that words are a major form of th electricity of the brain, then we can understand that different words have an impa on our bodies' chemistry and our ultimate emotions and behaviors. The proble is that we prefer to take the easy path and pretend that we are driven by the brain, rather than taking the more proactive role of getting into the driver's seat and choosing to create more of our reality. We **can** change our habitual ways of thinking as astrophysicist Carl Sagan states, "Habits are encoded in the brain, but they are also wired for change." Semantic realignment is one way of doing just this!

HOW TO USE SEMANTIC REALIGNMENT

The key to semantic realignment is to use verbs because they indicate action. Here are some examples of the nonproductive use of verbs that leads to negative self-talk:

I am **plus** any negative	I am fat, I am stupid,	Refers to the essence of what we **are**
I am not **plus** a positive	I am no longer thin, I am no longer confident	**I am** implies permanence
I can't	I can't dance or do math	Becomes our **reality**
I hate	I hate math and dancing	Becomes a **"chore"**
I have to, should, got to	I have to do homework rather than choosing	Implies being **"pushed"**
I must have/need	I need that car	Makes "wants" sound like imperatives **rather** than choices we desire

As soon as you use the term "I am" the brain recognizes it as the essence of who you are. It implies "permanence." Second, since verbs and nouns receive the most energy in programming, the brain does not always understand the confusing message of a negative plus a positive such as "I am not intelligent." When used with negative self-talk a lot of neuronal energy is generated that does not strengthen the self-concept. Add in "I can't" and you are telling your brain that you see your reality **one** way, which can have a negative impact such as saying "I can't do well." We often hear people proclaim "I can't understand science" or "I can't have a healthy relationship." This type of self-talk can seal the fate for the person using it, for they choose to not see life beyond their "can'ts."

Complicate matters by "hating" what you are doing and everything in life becomes one huge "chore." And finally, burden yourself with messages such as "I have to, should and got to" and you feel like the world is holding a gun to your head, forcing you to act. One young man expressed to us that he **is** an unlikable person. When asked why he felt this way he claimed "My parents tell me I'm really average looking. My older brother is so much smarter than I am and I don't have a lot of friends. I look at myself and I don't see anything that tells me I should fee differently. I **have to** believe the truth, don't I?" If we live, as this young man does with the sense that we "have to" think, act or feel a certain way, we never accep our own responsibility for our actions. The reality is that everything we do, every act and reaction, is a **choice** we make. No one is holding a gun to your head making you read this book. You have chosen to read it for specific reasons.

The same can be said for using "I must have" or "I need" statements. We create and communicate a feeling that implies we will "die" if our want or need is not met. Semantic realignment means acknowledging when we "want" something and owning that desire. Creating negative self-talk just makes the process harder There is not a magician in your brain who is saying, "well, we know that she doesn't mean that, let's surprise her." No, your brain believes the messages tha you give it whether they be positive or negative. So we end up placing self imposed limits on ourselves. When you "choose" or "want" to do everything in your daily life you begin to act out of a sense of freedom. In essence, you unlock one of your barriers.

Consider how history would change if everyone thought in these negativ patterns. It was once considered humanly impossible to run the mile in fou minutes or less. After Roger Bannister broke the four-minute mile barrier, withir a year fifty-two other men did too. As soon as people changed their interna program, they changed their external reality! Remember Mark Spitz, the grea swimmer of the 1976 Olympics who won 6 gold medals? So many swimmer throughout the world wanted to be the next Mark Spitz that within four year female swimmers in our Speech classes were equaling all his records and were sti not fast enough to qualify for the Olympics. Give yourself a fighting chance b telling your brain YOU CAN DO whatever you choose to do!

Have you ever studied hard for a test yet constantly worried that you "couldn't pass it? You may even have thought you knew the material, but when you took th test, you could not retrieve it. That is because when we say we fear something, ou brains are flooded with neuro-chemicals, such as adrenaline and dopamine, tha have the effect of morphine on the brain and shut down our ability to learn or t retrieve information. Whenever you are undertaking a test or a new challenge te yourself that you have faith in your ability to achieve your goal. You can do it!

To describe the effect of changing your "I am's" and "I can's," let us share wit you the success story of one of our students—a woman over 60—who had flunke math dozens of times. She had left math until the last course to take because of her fear of failure again. But she could not graduate until she passed math. Afte hearing about the use of the self-talk strategies, she wrote herself a new script an rehearsed it twice a day for three weeks. For two and one half weeks she wa worried that she was fooling herself and that the techniques of semantic realignmen were not working. She kept **those** thoughts to herself. She only verbalized that she was an expert at math and that Einstein himself was her tutor at night, etc. On the twenty second day, she was being tutored by her husband, who did not understand how to do a particular problem. All of a sudden, a *light* seemed to go on inside her head! She understood how to solve the problem and as the week progressed she was sure that she knew math now and could pass the final. Not only did she pass the final, she earned the highest grade in the class! Her husband was so proud of her achievement that he bought her a trip to Europe! Now if a 60 year old with a lifetime history of math failure could overcome this roadblock, just think what you can do to reprogram your self-talk!

It is important to realize that from wherever your "wants" converge, it is "your choice" from that point on. Remember, choice is a proactive term. Have you ever noticed how long an event is when you "have to" be there? And conversely, how quickly time passes when you are doing something you **want** to do? It is all in the attitude, and attitudes begin with the **words** you talk to yourself with.

To realign your language begin to use the following words instead of any negative messages you are currently in the habit of using:

I am plus a positive	I will/desire/want
I can/I do	I hope
I want/I choose	I have faith

Consistent use of semantic realignment will produce changes in how you feel, how your interact with others and, most importantly, how you view yourself.

HOW TO USE POSITIVE AFFIRMATIONS

A popular way to use semantic realignment for personal change is to create specific affirmations designed around concrete goals. These affirmations should be filled with the verbs listed above. Affirmations are written and spoken phrases that set up desired self-fulfilling prophecies we wish to create for ourselves. It is vital to remember that an affirmation needs to be stated in purely positive language. A good formula for constructing an affirmation comes from Stephen Covey, "*A good affirmation has five basic ingredients: it's personal, it's positive, it's present tense, it's visual and it's emotional.*" **DO NOT** use any negative language. For example, you would not state, "I am losing weight because I **no** longer eat sweets." Instead, you would affirm only the positive new habits of eating which will help you attain your desired weight. The new affirmation would be, "I am slim, healthy and physically toned."

Another important guideline for phrasing affirmations for maximum impact is to be sure to have an achievable goal and state the affirmation as if the goal has already been reached. It takes between three and six weeks to change a habit therefore affirmations are most effective if the goal can be reached in a six week period. If your desired goal will, realistically, take a year to achieve, break it down into smaller goals that feel less overwhelming.

Combining the Covey formula, as well as using a realistic goal, an affirmation would sound like the following:

I   *enjoy eating salads*   *filled with crisp, fresh vegetables.*

(personal) (positive, emotional, present tense)   (visual)

OR:

I   *jog easily and happily*   *every morning for 45 minutes.*

(personal)   (positive, emotional, visual)   (present tense)

In chapter two we discussed how one positive verbal statement creates enough "brain reaction" to neutralize up to 100 negative statements. So to supercharge the impact of these affirmations, say them out loud for at least 5 minutes, twice a day. Write your affirmations twenty times before going to bed each night to reinforce your positive changes as you sleep. Write them on small cards and attach them to mirrors, refrigerator doors and locations where you will see them and be reminded to say them throughout the day. Sing them in the shower or in your car while going to school or work. It is not advisable to sing them out loud in public places however—some people may wonder about you! One final insight, if you can say them while in front of a mirror it gives the visual part of your brain feedback that helps assist the programming. The more you make conscious use of affirmation the faster old habits will change and you will suddenly start viewing yourself in an entirely new light!

A FEW LAST "WORDS"

Thinking and speaking positively about oneself is hard for many people to do. For many of us it is a struggle. We have been taught not to brag, to be humble and to downplay any positive attributes about ourselves. It is even more damaging for individuals who have not received sufficient positive feedback in their lives for they become unable to reflect back a positive self-affirmation. Many people reach adulthood without having learned the difference between positive self-esteem and egotism. Yet, who would publicly admit to being "perfect" and not fear rejection for being conceited and self-centered?

One student openly shares a collage that represents his true self, trusting the growth that comes from mutual self-disclosure.

We are not asking you to become an egotist. We are suggesting that you simply learn how to **like yourself** more and become a more effective communicator through the use of positive self-talk. In the beginning it may feel as if you are "bragging" about yourself. Our reaction is SO WHAT! A little bragging can go a long way to help improve your self-esteem. You do not have to publicly advertise your positive characteristics. You simply need to take time every day to stop and listen to your current self-talk and, where it is unproductive or damaging, empower yourself by changing it. It won't take long to realize that the main person who has been talking badly about you is **you**! And you are the only person who can change **you**! So, have a little talk with yourself and watch the doors to self-awareness open wide!

Chapter Six
VISUALIZING NEW TERRITORY

*The Real Voyage of
Discovery
Consists Not in Seeking*

*New Landscapes but
in Having New Eyes*

— Anonymous —

attempt (v) to try to do sth, esp sth difficult.

asset (n) a useful or valuable quality, skill or person.

VISUALIZATION

Twentieth century man travels in two directions—outward to space and inward to the mind. Traveling outward he uses space craft, traveling inward he uses images...

At the edges of the universe inner and outer become one.

Mike Samuels, M.D. and Nancy Samuels

All great explorers know that the key to discovery lies in having a vision. Christopher Columbus might never have attempted to find the West Indies if he was not able to *see* in his mind its location in relationship to the rest of the world. Lewis and Clark would probably have stayed home if they had no images of the Northwest Passage. Our ability to visualize our past and our present, to imagine new ideas and creations is one of our greatest assets. Becoming explorers of our own visions opens up a new world of possibilities for growth. In her book *Teaching for the Two-Sided Mind*, educator Linda Verlee Williams stresses that this is "a door to our inner world, that magical realm where the imagination creates its own realities unfettered by the limitations we encounter in the outer world. Time and space pose no problem for the mind. Within it we can travel to China at the suggestion of the word or shrink to the size of an atom to explore microscopic worlds. It can allow us to become anything the mind can conceive of."

The purpose of this chapter is to explore visualization techniques which can open doors to growth. Through the use of proactive mental pictures you can change your understanding of yourself. Choosing more positive visual images of you and your life can lead to new worlds you've only dreamed of!

WHAT ARE VISUALIZATIONS?

Also called *imagery*, Adelaide Bry, in her book *Visualization—Directing The Movies of your Mind*, calls visualizations "movies-of-our-mind." Bry states, " movie-of-your-mind is a special kind of 'home movie' in which you are the screenwriter, producer, director, star and camera person. This home movie can go anywhere in time and space and can unreel any type of material you want to view. It comes to you uncensored, direct from the recesses of your mind, and is unfailingly accurate, interesting, and meaningful." You may believe you are not a "visualizer," but in truth your brain has been making mental pictures since the day you were born, and is constantly adding to your storehouse of visual memories. For example, just for a minute close your eyes and try not to think of a pink elephant with big green dots jumping on a trampoline. What happened? No doubt you had a visual image of this elephant! Word pictures can evoke the most unrealistic images. In fact, the word "imagine" means literally to "make an image." We normally have no problems recalling the "pictures" from our recent past. For example, do you remember where you parked your car this morning or afternoon? What color is it? Now, turn your attention to seeing your bedroom as you left it this morning? Was it clean or messy? Now, turn to your memories to your best friend in tenth grade. Could you see these images your mind's eye?

Our inner eye can also construct movies that we might desire to come true in the future. For example, imagine what it would be like for you to meet a favorite rock star? Or see yourself and a favorite person on a secluded beach in Hawaii—the sun is out, the warm gentle waves are lapping at your feet and love is in the air. Whether your images are clear as a bell, somewhat fuzzy, or even fleeting thoughts, you do have innate image-making abilities just waiting for you to spend more attention on them. So let us enter the door to the magical world of our inner movies.

CREATING VISUALIZATIONS

What follows is a step-by-step process for becoming your own visionary. Remember these are guidelines that open up limitless possibilities for applying visualization to your life!

Be In the Right Frame of Mind

Visualization works best when you are in a relaxed state. This will allow you to move away from the dominance of the left brain's processing and move toward the more slow "alpha brain wave" rhythm which encourages the right hemisphere to be active. It helps to be lying down with your eyes closed. Closing your eyes eliminates 70 percent of the incoming environmental information. Do not try to force the imagery—let it unfold along your general plot line, and be receptive to new and surprising images which may come up as messages from your subconscious. Remember, you cannot FORCE imagery from the right hemisphere, and trying too hard will block the natural flow. By choosing to feel positive about your visualizations you will enhance your physical and emotional experience.

crucial (adj) extremely important or necessary
inventive (adj) very good at thinking of new and original ideas.
evocative (adj) making u remember or imagine sth pleasant.

Unit Two: Further Explorations

Creative visualization is also more effective when you choose a "speciall designed," quiet place where you can stay in the relaxed state for at least 20 to 4 minutes at a time. Einstein would lock himself in his room and not even eat fo days when he was exploring the universe with his mind. He found that it wa crucial to limit as many distractions as possible.

film

Scripting Your Desires

As with any movie, it is essential to create a script set around an exciting plc line. In this case, the plot should be a positive, self-selected goal which can b achieved within a six-week period. Make sure that your goal is a "want" instea of a "should." Visualization works best when your mind and your heart are i agreement. In other words, what you choose to picture must be consistent wit your values. After choosing the plot-line, you can then imagine scenes where yo will see yourself actively achieving the goal. Be creative with your images and hav a positive attitude about the outcome.

Refining Your Script

Creative "movies-of-your-mind" help you utilize the inventive capacities of th (n) right hemisphere. As we learned in an earlier chapter, our mental pictures increas té bào thần neuronal energy and therefore prove the old saying that, "a picture is worth kinh thousand words." In fact, we recommend you begin refining your script by thinkin of your goal as an evocative "still" photograph, as if you have taken a picture of with a camera.   Next, close your eyes and begin to focus the picture of this "ne and better you" by doing the following:

1. Move your image closer to you.

2. If your image is in black and white, brighten it with some color.

3. Make the image brighter and bigger by adding more detail.

4. Remove any "frame" you have around your picture and make the edge endless.

5. Make your picture begin to move, adding activity. But always remember, yo are in control of the pace! Try making it into a musical performance, see you movie as a television show, a live dramatic performance or a cartoon.

6. Dramatize the fun and excitement of this goal by feeling the emotions you will experience when you have attained your goal in the "real" world.

7. If you want to overcome a negative image, feeling or situation that is keeping your growth blocked, reverse the process. Create a picture and make it far away, black and white, fuzzy focus, framed, still motion and with no excitement or energy! This will help you de-emphasize the emotional impact of a negative image.

Other Script Tricks

The more **vivid** the image, the more you energize pathways into the brain that help you to rapidly attain your desired goal. According Peter Russell's *The Brain Book,* experiments done on visual images and memory show that, "when the images were vague and indistinct, recall was around 70%, which was far higher than that gained by rote repetition. But, when the images were 'seen' vividly and distinctly, as if they were **real,** recall of learned information was around 95% PERCENT!"

The second most important element of the image, other than being vivid, is that it is an **interactive** one. As much as possible, you must **see** yourself as if your goal has been achieved. An interactive image has all elements working together. For an example of a vivid and interactive visualization, let us turn to one student who wanted to raise her grade in History class. She wrote this script for herself to visualize:

> *"Lori, as you begin to study History homework, you are relaxed and confident. Your mind is relaxed and ready to totally absorb all the knowledge like a dry sponge in a big bowl of water. You feel excited about all the fascinating new material you are reading. The pages come alive for you and are full of fun ideas and unique people from the past. You are stimulated by history and find it all so new and exciting. You feel as if you are living and experiencing the history as it is happening."*

With each new chapter she studied, Lori would incorporate the characters from history, see herself getting an A on all tests and learning history easily. It worked for her—she raised her grade from a C to an A minus in 5 weeks!

On a regular basis Lori successfully uses visualization while studying.

Another trick to stimulating the mental processes of the right hemisphere that whatever you are picturing must look "FUN" and "EXCITING." The "FLOW" state, which marks the use of the less dominant right hemisphere, is maintained when a state of **ease** and **enjoyment** is a main emotional component. The moment you make or see something as unexciting, a chore or requiring discipline, the more logical and detail-oriented processing of the left hemisphere will take over again, diminishing the impact of your imagery.

Just as in any blockbuster movie, your script should include a lot of action-oriented words and emotional overtones. Just be sure to select words that support the picture and the goal. The word-picture you create for yourself should also be in the present tense as if you are currently experiencing the image. Your right hemisphere has the working vocabulary of about a fifth grader. So, put away your Thesaurus and keep it simple but exciting. Stay away from vague, abstract qualities, such as "John Doe, you have the ability to be a good speaker." Instead create a more detailed picture such as "John Doe, as you speak to the huge crowd your lips are flexible, your mouth is moist, your words and ideas flow easily and freely. You feel as brilliant as Shakespeare. When you finish the crowd is giving you a standing ovation." Be sure and feel the excitement, see the crowd and hear the clapping hands. Experience this word picture with all of your inner senses and make it as real as you can. Dr. Samuels, co-author of *Seeing With The Mind's Eye,* notes the greater impact of action-oriented images by stating, "When a person holds an image in his mind he is compelled to participate in it's reality. All his senses are awakened. He sees, smells, hears, and feels more intensely." In other words the more your internal picture seems real, the more effective it will be in helping you change external reality.

VISUALIZATION AND ROLE REHEARSAL

Based on the research that says your nervous system does not know the difference between a vividly imaged internal event and a real external event sports psychologists have been using a technique called ROLE REHEARSAL. Visual training not only increases an athlete's confidence levels, it prepares him or her for the "real" event because it also directly affects the muscles of the body. It has been shown that when a person *imagines* an activity taking place in the body, electrical changes can be detected in the associated muscles of the body, despite the fact that the action is all "in the mind." Dwight Stone, the first person to jump seven feet, says that he pictured himself clearing the desired height hundreds of times before the actual event. Then the actual jump was just one more repetition of his "script." When you are using visualization, it is important to make the internal images as vivid and as intense as you can so that you trigger neuronal firing from the right brain and allow it to expand throughout your body. Consider for example, the 1988 Olympic champion diver, Greg Louganis. When he needed a perfect dive to win his second Gold medal, he became tense and misjudged the board. The world watched with horror as Louganis hit his head on the diving board. Many other athletes would have approached the final dive with a negative picture or fear of another mishap, but Louganis had been working seriously with visualization for many years. He returned to the diving platform, quieted himself on the board, saw the perfect dive in his mind, and then dove for a perfect 10! Through the "mental" edge that imagery gave him, he was able to overcome fear and create a place for himself in history!

VISUALIZATION AND HEALING

This connection between our images and our bodily reactions has also led to the increased use of mental imagery for medical purposes. Dr. Carl Simonton conducted research on cancer patients who used visualization as part of their therapy. Simonton taught patients how to actively visualize their bodies well Some young patients imagined their white blood cells joining with Luke Skywalke and "The Force" to successfully combat the cancer cells symbolized by Dart Vader. Those who incorporated visualization techniques with their regular medica therapy had a 30% complete recovery rate, and another 45% improved physically The greater importance of imagery in healing as opposed to using "just" words i stressed by Dr. Kenneth Pope of the Brentwood, California Veterans Administratio Hospital, "Telling your blood pressure to drop just doesn't do it, because verba language has a very limited impact on the autonomic nervous system. On the othe hand, "the autonomic nervous system does respond to the more basic language c IMAGERY, and is a vital aid to lowering blood pressure." From sports performanc to wellness, visualization is a very powerful tool.

SOME LAST WORDS ABOUT VISUALIZATION

It is important to create a visual landscape that is very vivid and involves a many of your five senses as possible. Since the right hemisphere is filled wit inventive capabilities and is largely non-judging, let your imagination run freel with your internal movies. It is not necessary to be realistic and logical. It is mor important that you have fun while stimulating the creative "genius" that resides i your right brain. At the age of 70, one of our students was tired of a lifetime c failure at math and wanted to rewrite her visual script to become a success at matl She had read about a Doctor in Tiburon, California who had freed many youn people from their learning disabilities by teaching them to visualize taking out the brains at night, washing them, and then returning them cleaned and smart. So sh did the same with one change. Following the brain-bath she visualized Einstei plugging his brain into her brain and filling it up with all his knowledge abou math! Her imagery worked. Within three weeks of working with this picture sh passed her math class with flying colors! So don't limit yourself to just wha might seem attainable and logical. Remember, there are no limitations in th universe of the right brain! You are the explorer and can draw your ma anyway that works for you!

Chapter Seven
DISCOVERING THE "WHOLE" YOU

WHOLE-BRAIN AND CONNECTED THINKING

A galaxy of stars, a vast galaxy continually twinkling on and off, with new stars lighting up. Think of your brain as a galaxy. See it filled with light. It's a galaxy beckoning us to explore.

Sheila Ostrander and Lynn Schroeder

Once a new territory has been explored, it has to be mapped so that one can find the way back and so that other adventurers can follow the same path. Mapping your journey into self-awareness will not only allow others to follow your example, but also allows you to reinforce your own learning. The more you work with the techniques in this book, the more your potential will expand. This chapter will help you take the next step by teaching you how to bring many of these techniques together so that you learn how to use your "whole" inner territory. Specifically, you will be adventuring into the "whole-brain" state, with all of its mysteries and magic.

WHAT IS THE WHOLE-BRAIN STATE

Previous chapters opened the doors to understanding how the two hemispheres of the brain influence the way we communicate. You found that "self-talk" will strengthen your connection to the verbal and analytic aspects of the left hemisphere. Visualization techniques open the doors to the creative realms of the right hemisphere. Now we will explore how to unify and awaken the best of both these worlds. MAGIC can occur when we link up these two diverse realms of "knowing" and choose to become greater than the sum of the parts. The process of accessing both hemispheres is referred to as "connected thinking" or "whole-brain learning." The term "whole-brain" refers to the state in which both hemispheres are synchronized. Think of this process as if a mirror is placed in the center of the brain. The electrical brain wave activity of one hemisphere is reflected and matched in the other. Much research is centering around the best ways to access connected thinking because we increase our physical, mental and emotional effectiveness from five to ten times when in this state. This accelerated process is often called "super-learning" or "super-performance." Using our imagination, having an interest in the inner self, listening to music and practicing relaxation, breathing, and meditation techniques have been determined to be methods that can help us reach the whole-brain state.

What are the learning advantages when you use connected thinking? Whole-brain or hemispheric synchrony, according to the *Brain/Mind Bulletin,* has been found to be a major key to the greater creativity of the "geniuses" of our past, such as Michelangelo, Edison and Einstein. In addition, the ability to switch rapidly between hemispheres in combination with performing well on typically left brain tasks seems to be the hallmark of all higher intelligence. For example, gifted children have a more profound switching ability between hemispheres. Neuroscientist Dr. O'Boyle stresses that we need to remember that all learning involves both hemispheres in dynamic interaction. Developing a "processing PARTNERSHIP" can place you at the greatest advantage in your communication interactions.

MUSIC AND CONNECTED THINKING

A major key to whole-brain learning is the brain's need for stimulation, novelty, "thrills," and challenge on a daily basis. Dr. Jerre Levy, one of the more renown specialists in teasing forth the secrets of the whole-brain experience notes that "The brain is built to be challenged. Complexity and challenge promote optimal functioning." Therefore, to enhance learning the first step is to engage both hemispheres. When there's not enough going on to spark both hemispheres, attention follows the path of least resistance, and an attitude of boredom can set in. Boredom shuts down memory retention, whereas challenge and "paying attention" builds good memory. Whenever we do simple tasks that only engage one hemisphere of the brain, our attention span will be low. Therefore, to accelerate learning, we should seek out "novelty" experiences, because, according to the book *Super-Memory,* the entire brain "WAKES UP" at novelty, at that which intrigues it."

Music has been found to be a valuable key to opening the greater resources of the brain. Master memory methods have found that music is best for stimulating and integrating the entire brain. Stanford researcher, Avram Goldstein found that, when measuring the brain's physical indicators of excitement, music registered the highest "thrill" rating—up to ninety-six percent! Compare that to a seventy percent rating for sex. More and more we are finding that music has a tremendous impact on the brain and the body. In fact, Dr. David Tame, author of *The Secret*

being expose : revealing secrets about someone/sth

Power of Music, notes that because the roots of the auditory nerves are more widel distributed throughout the brain and possess more extensive connections tha those of any other nerves in the body, "THERE IS SCARCELY A SINGLE FUNCTIO OF THE BODY WHICH CANNOT BE AFFECTED BY MUSICAL TONES."

Music then is a primary stimulus to the brain and body and "it's use to charg the brain, enhance memory and nourish the mind is one of the more promisin breakthroughs around," according to neuroscientist Dr. Alfred Tomatis. "You ears are the primary organ of consciousness. It is made not only for hearing, bu is also intended to provide charges of electricity to vitalize the body."

We would like you consider the impact of music on the brain and the body fron the fact that orchestral conductors live longer than most professionals. They als spend a large part of their waking hours exposed to classical music. Dr. Joh Diamond, author of *Your Body Doesn't Lie,* states "At the age of seventy, by whic 50% of American men are deceased, 80% of all orchestral conductors are not onl alive, but active and working." Music has also been found to positively affect bod metabolism, digestion, circulation, blood pressure, blood cholesterol level breathing rates, release of stress and muscular energy. All in all, being exposed t the right kind of music is an all around health tonic.

In addition to all the positive health benefits, it has also been determined tha music is the SINGLE input to the brain that synchronizes the two hemisphere Therefore, the incorporation of music can be a second vital key for whole-brai learning. Scientists are speculating that the reason music is the single integrativ input stems from the sheer complexity of the wholeness of music itself. Whe listening to music, the rhythm, words, beat, scales and mathematics are bein processed by the left-brain . . . whereas, the melody, pitch, harmony, creativit emotions, and synchrony of the musical compositions are being processed by th right-brain. The stimulating whole-brain aspects of music offer us a valuable to for self-development.

MUSIC AND LEARNING

So far, we have explored the general influence of music, yet not all types music are effective in helping our inner growth! Some sounds actually a disruptive to the brain and body. According to Dr. Tomatis, "What the youth today are looking for is stimulation of their brain. The trouble is that they are n taken up with charging (healthy) sounds, but with discharging sounds. In th music they play, there are no high harmonics. The more they play their musi the more tired they feel, and the more they are obliged to increase the intensit of their music."

Whole-Brain Connected Thinking

Time orientation

Orientation in space

Strategy of Peak Performance

Athletics ⟶ Creative fluid movement
rapid hand-eye coordination

Science

Repetition of writing

Inventive New Ideas

Nobel Prize winners

Einstein
Edison
Da Vinci

Art

Illustration
Realistic
Sculpture

Impressionistic
Art breaking set
Chagall, Dali

Music

Lyrics
math/beat
Rhythm

integrates both hemispheres simultaneously

Poetry
harmony
pitch
balance

Hemispheric synchronicity allows for an enhancement factor of 5 to 10 times greater memory, recall, sales, super-learning. It also allows for greater health and less retained stress.

Unit Two: Further Explorations

If some people are bombarding themselves so often with harmful types of music what are the more beneficial types which can aid us in opening the door to the whole-brain, super-learning state? The following standards are good to follow when selecting music:

1. Music used for super-learning is generally high-frequency music featuring compositions for string instruments, (such as violin, piano, harpsichord, guitar or mandolin).

2. The music should be slow—4/4 time or 3/4 time—and approximately 60 beats a minute.

3. The slow and rhythmic pace of the music allows our breathing and our heart rate to naturally slow down and resonate with the pace of the music.

4. This state of slower breathing and heart rate automatically takes us into a relaxed, but alert, brain wave state called **alpha**. During the alpha state the brain wave rhythm is around 7 waves per second. This has been found to be the most optimal for super-learning because it is an indicator of a decreased awareness of the external world.

5. Many specialists urge people to listen to this special music with headphones for maximum results. With the use of headphones, the music will move gently rhythmically back and forth between the hemispheres, allowing them to be in a simultaneous state. This alpha state is one which is most productive for guided imagery, affirmations, relaxation, and super-learning.

For the individual who is not an expert on music locating the best "super learning" music is an easy task. Dr. Alfred Tomatis and other "super-learning" experts most often recommend classical baroque music. Baroque has two effects on the body—it stimulates an active whole-brain state and it has seventy beats per minute. Your heart rate will naturally follow this beat which means your body will be in a "normal, resting heart rate" state. Baroque includes artists such as Vivaldi, Pachebel, Mozart, Bach, Handel, Haydn and Tchaikovsky. We have found however that some of our students do not like baroque music. Many "New Age" selections also create the same brain state. For example Steve Halpern's music has been specifically designed to create these "whole-brain" states in the body. Favorites are Study Suite, Anti-frantic Alternatives For Living, Crystal Suite. Other contemporary artists that focus on the healing, whole-brain music are Kitaro, Paul Horn, Vangelis, Windham Hill artists, just to name a few. A final, easy choice for music for super-learning is to use a soundtrack from your favorite movie, a soundtrack that has no words, but which you found emotionally uplifting.

It is important to experiment with the choice of music until you find the artists and the music which work best for you. It must feel relaxing, soothing and uplifting to YOU! As Valerie Stratton Ph. D., at Pennsylvania State University, notes, "Studies show that the most important factor in relaxation was a LIKING for the music." Another important component for music for super-learning use is that the music be long-playing, with no words or lyrics. This is so that the brain can stay synchronized. When lyrics are in music more emphasis is given to the left hemisphere analytical processing style and synchronization can be broken.

MUSIC AND MEMORY

Now that we are clear about the type of music to use for super-learning in the whole-brain state, what other applications are there? Have you ever noticed that when an "oldie" comes on the radio, even if you have not heard the song in years, you remember the words after the first several beats. Soon thereafter, you may even remember what you were doing the first time you heard it. It might evoke some old memories of a relationship—joy, hurt, or anger—depending on the relationship. This phenomenon points out the power of music to aid in memory. Information and emotions that are experienced while listening to music, can be retrieved at a later date if the same music is listened to again. Music is not just for entertainment anymore!

Using music to aid memory is a very simple process:

1. When sitting down to study or to learn a new skill, select a favorite baroque album or a movie soundtrack and put the music on at a barely audible level so it serves as a background sound.

2. Match the music to the emotional state that would best benefit what you are learning. For example, if you are working on something that seems difficult and you want to feel that you can triumph over all odds, perhaps you would play the soundtrack from the movie "Rocky."

3. Play the **same** music each time you return to work on a particular subject or skill.

4. When you want to retrieve information, such as for a test, simply play (or even hum to yourself if it is not appropriate to have music present) the same music you used when initially learning it.

Unit Two: Further Explorations

A Super-Learning Environment

To further enhance the impact of the "super-learning" music, follow thes[e] steps recommended by Ostrander and Schroeder:

1. Close your eyes and center your body and mind before you try to lear[n] something new. Most people find it is easiest to sit and begin slow, rhythm[ic] breathing for this "centering." One common technique is to breath in slowly t[o] the count of 4—hold the breath to the count of 4—and breath out to the coun[t] of 4. Easy enough to remember! Relaxing this way just naturally slows dow[n] the heart rate and that, combined with the music in the background, create[s] the optimal learning state of the whole-brain.

2. When you have relaxed and centered yourself through the breath, add i[n] positive self-talk. Affirm that you are smart and knowledgeable about th[is] particular subject. Tell yourself how **easy** this subject is for you because yo[u] are an "A" student and you **enjoy** learning. It is important for optimal learnin[g] that you feel good about yourself, your abilities, and your subject before you begin to study.

3. In this relaxed state, move into a memory (a vivid image) of the last time yo[u] successfully passed a test. Recapture the rush of adrenaline and the positiv[e] feelings from your past "peak performance" and combine this image and feelin[g] with your positive self-talk. Re-energize that feeling of TOTAL CONFIDENCE i[n] yourself.

4. If you wish to be more experimental, some super-learning instructors teac[h] their students to visualize an expert in the subject—it can be anyone dead [or] alive, real or fictional. Good choices to imagine for math and physics could b[e] Einstein, Edison for Engineering, Benjamin Franklin for American Governmen[t] Magic Johnson for basketball, etc. After you have your selected "expert[,]" imagine yourself connected to all their knowledge and abilities on this subjec[t] Feel yourself absorbing all their expertise. Visualize yourself in the futur[e] taking the **successfully** taking the test as if you were this person.

As you open your eyes and move to your study area, take with you the totali[ty] of your affirmations, imagery, and the feeling of your power and ability to lear[n] This is the context in which your whole-brain can be opened for a super-memo[ry] and super-learning state. When students have used these techniques the grad[es] of previously "poor" learners began to rival those of the so-called, "high achievers[.]"

sustain (v)(Continue): to cause or allow sth to continue for a period of time.

hippocampus(n): a part of the brain that is part of the limbic system and is important for memory.

Discovering the "Whole" You

A few more suggestions standard for sustaining optimal learning are: *adj (optimum): best most likely to bring success*

1. Take breaks in your study time whenever you are feeling tired or saturated. Research has found that the brain remembers the first and last portion of material studied in an unbroken period of time. So break up the time periods every 30 minutes or so.

2. Super-learners can incorporate the brain's connection of memory and smells by having incense or a scented candle burning in the room. Favorite smells awaken the hippocampus of the brain which further stimulates retention.

3. Whenever possible, do not disrupt your sleeping time by studying all night. New information is consolidated by the brain during REM dream stage. A good night sleep is important for full retention. It is sad, but true, that if you go to a party or drink after studying, then it reduces your retention of the studied material. *giữ lại*

Performing Under Super-Learning

Finally, on the day of the test use these easy techniques for accessing the "whole-brain":

1. Breathe to the count of 4—slowly and rhythmically. Enter the test location relaxed.

2. Allow the feeling of total confidence in your abilities to fill your body. An attitude of fear or anxiety tends to send out neurotransmitters which shut down the recall of information. Attitudes of faith and confidence open up the files of memory for faster recall.

3. **Imagine** your eventual success, and SMILE, which has been shown to send out endorphines which aid greater recall.

4. Recall the smells and the music you used while you were studying for this test.

5. With confidence and ease take the test **knowing** you will be successful.

6. If you happen to blank out on any question, all you have to do is breath to the count of 4, allow the melody of the specific musical background to flow through your awareness and any information you studied with music will come back to you.

Music is a powerful tool for increasing your abilities. As you find yoursel
having success with these tools, you will also find your self-confidence and self
esteem increasing.

BREATH AND THE WHOLE-BRAIN

Conscious, patterned breathing is a time-honored method to achieve whole
brain awareness, relaxation and to help memory. Different breathing technique
have been used in many different traditions worldwide. For centuries, Yogis hav
taught that to focus or fix something into memory, one should hold his breath fo
a minimum of seven seconds. The contemporary Japanese inventor, Yoshir
Nakamats, developer of the floppy disc, digital watch and 2,300 other patents, ha
received his "most creative new ideas" while holding his breath four or five minute
at a time at the bottom of his swimming pool. He says, "that the water pressur
forces blood and oxygen into my brain, making it work at peak performance
While your authors believe that this may be a very effective technique for Dr
Nakamats, there must be easier ways to focus the breath to restore the body to
whole-brain, healthy, creative state.

The yogic traditions have long taught that to live well certain things must b
done while breathing through one nostril or the other. In the last decade, scientist
at the University of California at San Diego and at the Salk Institute of Biologica
Sciences have verified this ancient teaching. We now know that humans have 9
minutes to 2 hour cycles when one nostril is dominant over the other. Furthermore
they found that when you are breathing through your left nostril, your right brai
is dominant. Likewise, when breathing through the right nostril, your le
hemisphere dominates.

Researchers from Dalhousie report that people's verbal and spatial abilit
"varied markedly" with the rise and fall of brain dominance. Verbal ability ros
when the left brain was dominant. Spatial ability improved when the right cycle
up. We can therefore use the nose to fine tune the brain. When you desire mor
creativity, the key is to close off your right nostril and breath deep through the le
nostril—this opens up and energizes the right brain processing. If you are writir
a term paper, periodically close the left nostril and open up the left brain b
breathing in through the right nostril. You control which hemisphere is dominar
by which nostril is dominant.

Ostrander and Schroeder point out, "We are designed to oscillate betwee
action and rest . . . It's a life rhythm, one we often override." Yet, it is important n
to force dominance into one hemisphere for long periods of time. Like so much als
in nature, these "nostril" cycles reflect a larger natural rhythm cycling through th
whole-body and mind. When we override this natural rhythm, we tend to ove
emphasize one hemisphere. Selectively using this cycle by becoming more awa
and balanced in this breathing rhythm can assist memory, relaxation and increa
self-awareness.

A technique for helping to re-balance the natural cycle of breathing is referred to as "conscious alternate nostril breathing." Close off the right nostril first and breath in for a slow count of 8. Hold the breath for 4 counts feeling the lungs filled with energizing and cleansing power. Now switch and close off the left nostril and breath out slowly to the count of 8. Continue this process for several minutes, always remembering to switch nostrils before you exhale. After you have finished the conscious breathing cycle, rest with your eyes closed and tune into the body and its sensations. Before long you will be come aware of a feeling of being balanced again.

BREATH AND KINESTHETIC AWARENESS

Many of us are not very aware of our body sensations or our feelings. Our breath can be a key to releasing body tensions that can accumulate after a difficult situation and can also help dispel the residue of an unbalanced day. If you focus on your breathing patterns you will notice that whenever you feel tense, changes will occur in your breathing patterns. Generally speaking, the more stressed we are, the more shallow our breathing will become. Because of this short breathing pattern, we can feel tight in our chest, as if we **can't** take a full breath. Dr. John W. Travis and Regina Ryan, stress in their book, *Wellness—Small Changes You Can Use to Make A Big Difference*, that "adult humans normally breath at the rate of one breath every six to eight seconds and inhale an average of 16,000 quarts of air each day. If nothing is done to restrict the breathing it will happen naturally and fully. But people continually inhibit natural breathing in many ways—poor posture, tight or binding clothes, speed-eating, . . . smoking, and lack of exercise, plus habitual patterns of emotional stress all have a negative effect." This is why every approach to relaxation and whole-brain enhancement includes attention to breathing patterns. Take a moment now to close your eyes and tune into your body and its feelings. Then use this breathing technique:

1. As you inhale, imagine that you are breathing increased life, energy and joy into the areas that feel tired, painful, tight or in any way "starved."

2. As you exhale, imagine that all tiredness, pain, and negative energy leaving your body.

3. Repeat this "in-out" process until you feel refreshed and renewed. At least three to five minutes.

To increase the overall effectiveness of your breath work, Dr. Travis suggest you combine affirmations in this next breathing exercise:

1. Close your eyes and pay attention to your breathing for a moment or two.

2. Inhale, and as you do say to yourself, "I am" Exhale, and as you do, say t yourself: "relaxed." (or energized, or joyful or whatever emotion or sensatio you wish to program into yourself)

3. Continue repeating, "I am" with each inhalation, "relaxed" with eac exhalation.

4. Let your breathing gradually become a little deeper, a little slower, but don force it in any way. Just watch it happening. As your mind begins to wande gently bring it back to the awareness of breath and your affirmation.

5. Notice the overall positive effects of relaxation throughout your body.

Once you begin paying attention to your breathing patterns, you will notice tha there are times when you stop this natural cycle of breathing, especially in times strong emotion. Michael Sky states, "in fact, the most basic and automatic human reactions to aroused feelings is to tighten the body and constrict th breath." We do it because it is an effective short-term strategy for dealing wit unwanted feelings. Feelings are comprised of energy, and energy flows through th breath. Anytime we constrict our breath even slightly, we are diminishing th movement of energy throughout all levels of self. When we 'turn down' the volun of energy, we are also turning off our awareness of feeling. If we are not taught resolve these contractions of breathing deeply, and allowing our energies expand, "it can turn into a wound in our emotional body."

If all of our cycles can be observed as a give and take between movement ar rest, then we can see why the way that we breathe can be an excellent metaphor f the way in which we live our lives. It is crucial to a fully functioning and healtl body and mind that we focus on our breathing each day.

MEDITATION AND THE WHOLE-BRAIN

Breathing patterns and relaxation form the basis of the final important whol brain activity which is vital to our health and well-being—the practice of meditatio and contemplation. By applying all the techniques of this chapter you can learn go beyond the chatter of your own inner voice. Here you can enter a space whe you are at your best physically, mentally, emotionally and spiritually. Meditatic practices can bring this altogether for you.

to open inner doors

men of many races and times

have used meditation magic prayer

as we now use science to open

doors outwardly

how shall you open your doors?

       Paul Reps

    Although meditation traditions are centuries-old and practiced in almost every religion, it is because of the research on transcendental meditation and the "relaxation response" by Dr. Herbert Benson of Harvard Medical School, that modern medicine has studied the numerous beneficial aspects of meditation. Let us examine the major benefits we can gain if we meditate daily.

    Meditation involves quieting the body and the mind by focusing attention on a single source of unchanging input. As was discussed in earlier chapters, the body, mind and emotions represent an ongoing, closed-circuit communication feedback system. Meditation is a suggested pathway to re-balance all the seemingly separate parts of the body and mind as well as open a doorway to clearer self-communication.

    Researchers at the University of California at the Irvine Medical Center found that the practice of transcendental meditation (TM) increased the flow of blood to the hemispheres of the brain by 65% more than participants who were merely relaxed. This greater flow of blood supply may account in part for the many studies that show meditation improves mental performance and IQ levels up to 5 IQ points in two years. Meditation has also been found to be very beneficial to overall health and happiness. Fortune Magazine reported in August, 1988, that "people over 40 who spent twenty minutes twice a day using TM had 74% fewer doctor visits and 69% fewer hospital admissions than a control group who did not.

    Researchers over the last three decades have documented the many physiological benefits gained by daily meditators. Dr. Herbert Benson, Director of the Mind/Body Medical Institute of Harvard Medical School, has shown that building meditation or relaxation techniques into one's life reduces stress related diseases such as headaches, high blood pressure, and sleep disorders in particular. In addition, they found that both hemispheres of the brain and their mental abilities functioned at a higher level, although the body stayed at a deeply restful state.

Even more surprising, follow-up studies indicated that even after a meditation session ends, the benefits of meditation carry over into the physical and psychological aspects of the your life. Meditators find it easier to cope with stress, experience more energy, and relief from fatigue, enjoy more confidence in their abilities and are more creative in their approach to problem-solving.

Using Meditation

There are as many different approaches to meditation as there are people who want to meditate. However, we will list the more highly researched methods and recommendations:

1. **Environment:** Almost all styles of meditation require a calm environment where you can lie or sit for 20 to 30 minutes undisturbed. Since the main purpose is to get the mind as "still" as possible and turn the focus of the brain from outward stimuli to an inward focus, it is vital that the place you pick be as quiet and noise-free as possible.

2. **An Internal Focus**: The second requirement is to shift the mind from external thoughts to an internal focus. This is done by closing the eyes, and choosing a "centering device"—a constant point of focus. Since one of the aims of meditation is to quiet the "ongoing chatter of the mind," most meditation styles select something to break up the ongoing train of distracting thoughts, typical of "mind-wandering" when the mind is not engaged from exterior stimuli. Centering devices could include:

3. **The Breath**: Follow the path of inhalation and exhalation as it travels through your body. If you start thinking about anything else, or lose track of your breath, just notice this and return your awareness to the flow of breath in and out. Generally, the breath is completed through the nose. Although, you can experiment with the differences of breathing through the mouth first and then moving to breathing through the nose. It is a different experience for the brain and body. Dr. Herbert Benson recommends combing this with the word "ONE,"

    "Breathe through the nose. Become aware of your breathing. As you breathe out, say the word, "ONE" silently to yourself. For example, breathe IN, OUT, "ONE"; IN....OUT, "ONE": etc. Remember to breathe easily and naturally. Continue this for 10 to 20 minutes."

4. **Passive Acceptance**: The third requirement is to maintain an attitude of passive acceptance. You can be sure that as you start to meditate a myriad of distractions will occur. Don't fight them or struggle with them. Instead just let any thoughts rise and fall or float away, like leaves on a stream. As you notice any distracting thoughts, just easily return to your "centering" device. Just repeat the word or phrase and allow your mind to swing out again into the universe of the inner mind. Consider the centering device as the core of a spiral. Each time the thoughts return, your centering device can spiral your inward focus onward.

5. **Mantra**: A mantra is generally a Sanskrit word or syllable with special spiritual significance. A mantra can be repeated silently or chanted out loud. Basically, this idea follows the procedures of Benson's "relaxation response" with a mantra being used instead of "ONE." Common mantras include "ram," "amen," "OM" or "AUM." One system includes chanting the vowels of the English alphabet and imagining a specific color with each vowel. Choose whatever feels **right** to you. The purpose of the mantra is to focus the mind, so that one can still the ongoing "chatter of the mind."

6. **Affirmations**. Some people use phrases or affirmations to stay centered while meditating. This helps instill the qualities that they are affirming. Some suggestions are "I only feel love," "I am relaxed and happy," or "I am full of peace."

Mindfulness Meditation

The practice of "mindfulness," used particularly in Zen traditions, takes a slightly different focus. The intent here is to stay fully aware of your "present moment" without the distraction of random thoughts Whatever you are doing you do with an attitude of total absorption in your moment to moment awareness. A teacher of mindfulness, Dr. Kabat-Zinn, notes that "without realizing it, most of us routinely waste enormous amounts of energy in reacting automatically and unconsciously to both the outside world and our own inner experiences . . . but all of us have the capacity to be mindful. All it involves is cultivating our ability to pay attention to the present moment. The path to it in any given moment lies no farther than your own body and mind and breathing."

Unit Two: Further Explorations

One method of mindfulness is to act as if you are "witnessing" what i going on, as if you are a separate person with no investment in the person yo are observing:

1. Notice the breath and the rhythmic rise and fall of your abdomen.

2. Now expand your awareness to the full range of sensory thoughts, feelings an perceptions.

3. Note your posture, body sensations, taste, muscular tensions, as well a sensations outside the body, such as the feel of air moving about the body, th sounds you hear, the temperature of the room, etc.

4. Watch yourself with no judgment.

Contemplation

In the Judeo-Christian tradition, the meditative practice is referred to a contemplation. The main purpose is to seek the power of silence in order to be ab to "hear the still, small voice inside," the intuition or the voice of conscience. Th is the sound one mystic has referred to as "the Spirit of Life that is always speakir to our souls." Sally Olds reinforces the great need for contemplative silence whe she states, "Only in silence can we hear the voice of the soul, when we're bus talking, or preparing to talk, we're deaf to the songs within us. We also see thing more clearly when we're not distracted by talking or listening to talk. . . . Durir silence your thoughts are quieter, deeper, more seed-level. You're giving yourself, helping yourself. . . . Silence is the cheapest therapy in the world. The ro of therapy is self-observation, and silence creates a sanctuary for this."

How can we use contemplation to gain greater insight into our self-awarenes Use the following steps:

1. In order to gain access to your inner wisdom through contemplative meditatio you first need to be quiet. A very still silence. Any of the previously discusse methods will help you achieve this silence.

2. After the body and mind are steeped in silence, pose a simple and dire question—a question that can be answered in one or two simple phrases.

3. After posing the question, simply stay open and receptive and listen for an answer to come from your inner voice. The information can come in many different forms, words, images, symbols, sounds, an inner knowing, song lyrics, feelings, energy, or any other number of subtle ways. "In contemplation," Robbie Gass reminds us, "the information you are asking for already exists: you are not figuring it out, but rather just connecting to it."

YOUR WHOLE-BRAIN

Through the next several decades we will be seeing an increasing number of techniques designed to allow us to use the whole-brain state. Educators, health care providers, spiritual organizations and everyday people will increasingly reap the benefits of this incredible frontier. We are just beginning the tap the riches available to us within our own inner treasury. By using the methods in this chapter you are drawing your own map into these uncharted realms. As you develop your self-awareness, others will follow. It is part of our evolutionary development. Enjoy the journey!

Chapter Eight
LISTENING TO
YOUR INNER GUIDANCE

BODY AWARENESS AND DREAMS

The more faithfully you listen to the voice within you,

the better you will hear what is sounding outside.

Dag Hammarskjold

Communicating from the inside out truly means becoming the explorer of our own inner resources. Listening to the people around us becomes far more productive when we have taken the time to *listen* to ourselves, to *tune* into our internal processing and to learn how to use our own inner wisdom in our daily lives. We generate messages from a variety of internal resources. In our waking states, our bodies continually send us information about our interaction with other people and the environment. Even when we sleep we are constantly processing input, problem solving and examining our lives. The more skilled we become at understanding and using this information, the more effective we will be in our lives. This chapter will address several methods we can use to *tune* into the "inside" so we can become more aware of the "outside."

LISTENING TO OUR BODIES

In an earlier chapter we discussed the way the brain processes auditory and visual inputs. Self-awareness does not stop there—it travels the full length of the body. Kinesthetic inputs refers to the way we process information physically. literally stands for those moments when we do not *hear* or *see* information as part of our thought processes, but rather when we *feel* them in our bodies. Have you ever experienced the memory of a painful event and you felt this recollection by "replaying" the physical sensations of the actual event? Perhaps your stomach tightened up, you became short of breath or felt pressure in your head. By listening to your body you can learn to understand your own unique kinesthetic processes and use that information in future events. Furthermore, by exploring the "triggers" of your physical reactions, you can change the **way** you react, and thus change the way you communicate.

90

Why should we listen to our kinesthetic messages? Psychotherapy research has shown that people who improve listening to their own bodies gain greater insight and direction into problems and conflict situations than individuals who attempt to solve problems through thinking **alone**. If you are exercising and a body part begins to hurt, it would be wise to respect that message by stopping what you are doing. Likewise, it would benefit you to listen to all of your kinesthetic messages and pay attention to their impact on self-awareness. Nicole, an eighteen year-old student, continually had pain in her stomach. After suffering with this condition for over a year she finally sought medical help where she was diagnosed with a bleeding ulcer. It was only after she was told to radically change her diet and was given three prescription drugs that she decided to listen to this body message. Through some self-exploration she realized that her pain was at its worst whenever she had a test or paper due at school. She already knew that she had "perfectionist" tendencies and that her family demanded that she get superior grades. However, it wasn't until she faced a change in her life style that she recognized how she was storing the stress and pressure in her body. By acknowledging the information she was receiving from the kinesthetic level, by learning techniques to tune into her body daily and by changing the way she was **internally** processing her external life, she quickly found she could reduce her pain. Within several months she was eating "regular" food and felt healthier than she had in a very long time.

What Is Your Body Trying to Say?

We ask at this point that you be willing to be more than open minded, and literally **open** your body awareness that you might learn more about how you are interacting in your life. To do this we suggest the two following approaches for getting in touch with your kinesthetic "inputting." One deals with how the body stores information physically and the other explores the way in which emotions are stored in the body. The first is the **Body Scan**. Body scanning involves getting in touch with the physical state of your body and using that information to help you understand how you are interacting in your life. Use the following steps to do a Body Scan:

1. Sit in a quiet location, undisturbed with your eyes closed.

2. Take a moment and scan your body, starting at the head and moving your attention downward through your neck, shoulders, arms, chest, back, stomach, hips, thighs, calves and feet.

3. As you scan pay special attention to any points where a sensation exists. For example you may feel tension, tightness or tingling. Do not spend time thinking about any individual sensation—simply observe it and move on.

4. When you have finished your body scan return your attention to those points where you were aware of sensation.

5. Ask yourself "what am I feeling at this point?" Perhaps it is anxiety, excitement or the warmth of a moving energy.

6. Return your attention to the external situation and compare your body information to what is actually going on. Does the awareness of your kinesthetic response help you understand your role or situation better? Does it help you decide how to communicate by understanding your internal reaction?

The Body Scan can be used any time, in any situation and only takes a couple of minutes to complete. A process that takes a little more time and can help you delve even deeper was first introduced by Eugene Gendlin of the University of Chicago and is called **Focusing**. Focusing can be used to explore a problem, a relationship or a decision by getting in touch with how it "feels" in your body. Instead of thinking or talking about an issue this technique allows you to identify the emotions involved. It can help you examine what therapist Joseph Tein call "the difference between knowing with words and knowing with your body."

Also called "experiencing," this style of body awareness happens when you bypass mental processes such as rationalizing and intellectualizing and tune in to how important issues feel in your body. One opportunity to tune in to your body is when you are having difficulty putting what you are feeling into words. This indicates that you are not processing at a mental level. Here is an opportunity to begin to understand your own The next time this happens try the following method

1. Sit quietly, with your eyes closed.

2. Pick one problem to deal with and begin to think about it in general terms.

3. Now move your awareness from thinking and shift it into your body. Notice how you feel about the whole issue in your body. Clearly differentiate between **thinking** and sensing the **feeling** here.

4. Don't try to "second guess" what you're feeling. If you have decided

what your emotional level is ahead of time you will block new kinesthetic information. Allow what is in your body to "come up" and be open-minded about these discoveries. If these feelings make you uncomfortable, honor your resistance. Do not force this process.

5. If words come to mind, check to be certain that they match what you are feeling. If they do, then you are on the right track.

6. Ask yourself "what is this feeling communicating to me?" "What in this situation makes me feel this way?"

7. Keep **focused** on the sense of what you are **feeling**. Make sure you are not returning to a rational, intellectual process. As you stay focused you will begin to experience what Gendlin calls a "felt shift," a sense of a physical and psychological release, a loosening of both your emotions and your body. When this happens you will often gain new, fresh insights into the situation.

You can use this method **any time** you want to gain a greater understanding of your inner processes. There are times, however, when you may be experiencing conflict at such an intense level that you have a difficult time tuning into your body messages. You might not even be aware of this information at a conscious level and therefore unconsciously store it in the body. Massage therapists are keenly aware of this phenomenon. When people experience an intense emotion that is too powerful to deal with consciously, they often unconsciously store it in the muscle structure where it may persist for years. It can cause physical pain and present blocks to growth. Specialists in techniques such as emotional release massage use methods designed to help clients become aware of these emotions by finding where they are stored in the body, and then help these clients release this pent-up energy. Following a massage session, a young woman told one of your authors "It was amazing! The therapist started working on a muscle knot and, for an unexplained reason, I suddenly felt like crying. She continued to work, gently talking to me and before long I was sobbing harder than I have done since I was ten years old. I suddenly realized that the emotions I was experiencing were tied to being sexually abused at that age. I have never before felt such a release!"

Once you begin to grasp the way information moves in your body you can make choices about how to use it. If you know you are *feeling* anxiety you can choose how to express it. Negatively using the energy behind the anxiety can hurt the communication climate. We often hear students express that they "cannot control anger—it just rushes out!" Intense emotions do not have to overwhelm you. Through the use of techniques such as body scanning, focusing and massage you will learn where you experience emotions in your body. Once you have the have this greater self-awareness, you can choose to deal with these emotions more positively.

LISTENING TO THE SUBCONSCIOUS MIND

Many of us are fascinated by what the brain is doing when we are paying th
least amount of attention to it—that is when we are sleeping. Our dreams offer a
entire treasure chest of information about our desires, fears and frustrations tha
when applied to our conscious states, can help us be more effective communicator
You spend an average of 220,000 hours in your lifetime asleep. What is going o
and how can you take advantage of that time?

First, dreams do not occur throughout this unconscious state. On the averag
they occur 5 to 8 times a night during REM sleep (Rapid Eye Movement.) At th
point your brain waves stop sending messages to your spinal cord and you ar
virtually paralyzed, which keeps you from acting out the dream. Founder of th
Maimonides Hospital Dream Lab, Dr. Montague Ullman, describes dreams thi
way, "The dream is a function of the waking state. When we waken we pull bac
part of the experience of dreaming. Pulling back and remembering the dream is a
attempt to communicate, through language, an experience which has occurred i
a different mode, a pictorial mode. The initial dreaming experience undergoes
transformation. During the process some information is lost."

So, what are dreams trying to teach you? Barbara Levine, in her book You
Body Believes Every Word You Say, explains that dreams provide "an altere
experience of reality, a different time and space reference." They seem to be
stress release and crisis periods seem to highlight the lessons we can learn whe
listening to our dreams. According to Dr. Rosalind Cartwright and Lynne Lambe
in Psychology Today, when we are experiencing pressure "our dreams go into hig
gear . . . we search our life story to find memories that can help us cope. We slee
more lightly and awaken more often. Dreams are more apt to stick with us whe
we are troubled than when life is going well."

Sleep deprivation also has a large impact on our dream life. Psychologi
Carlyle Smith at Canada's Trent University found that students who disrupt RE
sleep by partying all weekend forget much of what they learned during the wee
There seems to be a link between memory and REM sleep. "Dream" sleep appea
to be critical in permanently memorizing new skills. It is very clear that dream tim
has a great impact on our conscious and unconscious states.

What Do Dreams Teach Us?

Learning how to interpret your dreams can lead you into a maze of books an
information. As varied as this information can be, there is general agreement tha
dreams fall into several categories. Cartwright and Lamberg have found that th
most common dream dimensions are the following: safety versus dange
helplessness versus competence; pride versus shame; activity versus passivit
independence versus dependence; trust versus distrust; and defiance versu
compliance. We, your authors, both actively use dream interpretation in ou
own lives but agree with Sigmond Freud who believed that, whatever th

method used, if the interpretation makes no sense to the dreamer, then it has no purpose. So, it is important to find an interpretation guide that works with your values and philosophies.

Dreams can also have a "carry over" effect into our communication by influencing our moods. On student expressed that he had been having constant fights with his girlfriend due to a dream he'd had about her the previous week. In the dream he caught her in a secret relationship with another man. The dream was so vividly real that he awoke extremely "agitated" and had not been able to shake these feelings. Both at a subconscious level (the dream) and at the kinesthetic level (the feelings) he was receiving information about his relationship with her. Unfortunately, he was not dealing with this information productively and instead was allowing the emotional "backwash" of the dream to create even more conflict for him.

So, the first and most obvious step to begin "listening" to your dreams is to *remember*, them. To help in remembering your dreams use the following suggestions:

1. Keep a pen and paper by your bedside to make notes of any images, thoughts or feelings you have upon waking. You can also use this "dream diary" during the daytime to keep track of events and concerns that could have a relationship to your dreams.

2. Before going to sleep at night, tell yourself you **will** remember a dream. Some people even set their alarm clocks to match their sleep cycle so they will be awakened during REM sleep.

3. When you wake up lie still with your eyes closed and start recalling your dream. Staying in this "twilight" state can help you with dream recall, while opening your eyes and getting right up can push images further away from consciousness . . . translate your pictures into words before opening your eyes.

4. Write down whatever comes to mind even if it is only a few words or thought fragments. You never know—several days later they may suddenly make sense!

5. Take whatever symbols, images or words you have recorded and ask yourself the following questions:

   "What is this dream trying to teach me?"

   "What events in my life does this dream relate to?"

6. If no dream images or impressions arise write down whatever you may be feeling emotionally or physically. Your dreams may have led to your conscious thoughts which could possibly provide you insight later on.

caliber (n) (quality) the degree of quality or excellence of sth or some

Unit Two: Further Explorations

7. If you only remember a fragment of your dream, think about the fragment a
    you fall asleep the following night. Often the details will come back full
    the second time.

8. If you cannot seem to remember your dreams try sleeping late on the weekends
    Extending your REM periods will extend the length and complexity of you
    dreams.

    Dreams are powerful tools for self-exploration. Taking the time to listen to the
messages allows us to truly learn "around the clock." We become explorers of th
highest caliber when we move beyond our waking experience and take an interes
in our *whole* experience.

> I am a dreamer
> amidst the dream
> come walk with me
> perhaps you'll see
> the dream i dance
> within
>
>   Mike Post*

Your Day and Night Messages

    We must also consider the
differences between our daydreams
and our night dreams when trying
to listen to these inner messages.
Interestingly enough, both share
many commonalties. Daydreams
and night dreams seem to follow a
single ninety-minute cycle that
continues around the clock.
Daydreams reach their peak about
every 90 minutes, while sleeping
dreams occur at about the same
interval. According to psychologist
Chuck Loch the right hemisphere
has a natural processing advantage
during these periods. The verbal
processing of the left brain is

*Printed with Permission by Michael Post

96

reduced while the visual processing of the right brain becomes dominant. Learning to recognize the onset of the daydreaming cycle as you go through your day can help you make the most out of your brain power for this marks an opportunity for creative thinking.

Daydreams are equally valuable sources of information that, as Dr. Eric Klinger explains, "are part of our internal information system, our internal self-housekeeping and self-management system." We spend an average of half of our mental activity on some kind of daydreaming and can actively use this time to increase or self-awareness. Controlling your daydreams can be used to help you relax in a tense situation such as when you go to the dentist.

You can use them as a mental calendar to help you keep tabs on your schedule or upcoming issues. And you can look at the issues that come up in your daydreams to help you determine what is important in you life right now. Klinger states that, "Mostly they are about something you want or fear . . . whether it is staring you in the face or buried below the surface meaning of the daydream, the object of your fear or desire is there."

RECORDING THE MESSAGES WE HEAR

The last tool we will discuss is easy to do—it just requires commitment. This method is journal-keeping and, when regularly used, can provide incredible insight into our inner processes. Journal-keeping can be done two ways. First and most obvious, is recording your thoughts, feelings and reactions on paper. Second, is recording this information on a tape player. Which ever system you choose, make sure you can conveniently carry your journal material with you so that you can record whenever circumstances and time allows.

Journal-keeping is an exceptional way to more fully process your reactions to the people and events in your life. Your journal can also tell you about your patterns, moods and cycles. Robert Thayer, a psychologist at California State University, Long Beach, has found through his research that specific patterns become very apparent through journal-keeping. For example, our moods and energy levels vary a lot during the course of a day. A problem we may feel optimistic about at mid-morning may seem like an insurmountable barrier by mid-afternoon. The problem has not changed, but our mood and willingness to put energy into it has.

Recording your experiences, especially more troubling or traumatic ones, can have a tremendous impact on your perceptions and physical health. Psychologist James Pennebaker studied the impact of journal-keeping on college students. Over four consecutive days students were asked to write about painful experiences. During the process many of them experienced intense emotions such as anger and guilt. However, by the end of the project, many of the students found they had a better understanding of the experience because journalizing had allowed them to organize their thoughts and assign meaning to the situation. The effect of writing was long lasting—four months later the students showed improvement in their mood and general outlook. What is the most interesting is that Pennebaker has found that people who write about powerful experiences also experience improved health. When you experience conflict, you often experience stress which weakens the immune system and leads to illness. Additional studies found that students who wrote about their conflicts had their T-cells, the cells in the immune system that fight infections, improve in efficiency. This improved physical state lasted up to six weeks beyond the initial journalizing. Journal-keeping allows you to understand your situation better, but also has the added benefit of acting like a prescription that helps heal your physical wounds as well as emotional wounds.

For journal-keeping to be successful you must be willing to review what you have recorded on a regular basis. This will allow you to evaluate your original perception on different issues in comparison to the current state of affairs in your life. It will also allow you to measure your growth as you continue on the path of discovery. One of your authors dramatically learned the value of journalizing when she was actively working with her dreams. One night she dreamed that a man was pouring water into her left ear. She kept saying "No, no!" Her left ear had been damaged years earlier and the thought of someone further interfering with it was frightening. The man in the dream just kept reassuring her that "it would be better." The following night she dreamed that she was given a beautiful purple Porsche *and* a gold Mazerati! A psychologist friend told her a few days later that the dreams obviously were telling her to "listen better and you will get wonderful results." It wasn't until a year later, when she **reviewed** the journal entries about these dreams that she realized how true the messages had been. In the course of that year her hearing had been restored and she was, once again, experiencing the world more fully!

COMMITMENT TO LISTEN

continuey
◊ keep doing it

Listening is hard work, whether it be listening to your own inner messages or to other people. It requires energy and commitment. We cannot force you to listen to your own personal guidance and wisdom. We just know that when people invest the time into this endeavor they grow further and faster than other people do. We are wondrous beings. The question is are we ready to be the explorers of our own inner frontiers!

Chapter Nine
THE WORLD IS YOURS

FEAR, RISK TAKING
AND FORGIVENESS

*Oh, the miraculous energy that flows between two people who
care enough to get beyond surfaces and games, who are willing
to take the risks of being totally open, of listening, of responding
with the whole heart. How much we can do for each other.*

Alex Nobel

Choosing to be an explorer leads to a natural consequence—before you realiz
it you have become a discoverer! Through the course of this book you have bee
given tools for mining the riches of self-awareness. As you unearth the treasure
within you, you face the choice all great discoverers face—what to do with your nev
knowledge. As you have found the keys to open the locked doors to self-esteem an
the greater use of your inner abilities, what will you do with this new persona
power? Many of you may find that you still have some fear about applying thes
skills in your life. Change is one of the greatest challenges we face. Yet, a
emotionally and mentally healthy person welcomes change for it is like having a ke
to the buried box of treasure. And when we open that box, our personal wealth ca
finally overflow and touch those we love.

The purpose of this chapter will be to examine the last steps to greater sel
awareness. We will explore what it means to face fear, to take risks, to forgiv
ourselves and to finally accept "who" we truly are.

FEAR CAN BE A FRIEND

Recently a student, looking very troubled, came to one of our offices. Whe
asked what was wrong, he explained that he was not certain he could complete
major class project. The project required him to look, from a variety of perspectives
at an old, painful memory. The goal of the assignment was to learn methods fo
releasing previous experiences that blocked new growth. This young man seeme

unable and unwilling to even consider attempting the process. Upon further discussion he finally revealed his true feelings, "I'm afraid of what I might learn about myself. I'm afraid of what I might learn about my past. And, I'm afraid about how this might affect my future." In other words, he was paralyzed with fear, absolutely cemented to the present with little hope to overcome this sense of panic unless he became willing to face it.

This student's feelings are not exceptional. On the contrary, they are commonly shared by many people. Can you name one person who is absolutely "fear free?" Probably not, and that means that fear is not an exception. Instead, fear is often the rule! Lloyd Jones once stated that "those who try to do something and fail are infinitely better off than those who try to do nothing and succeed." Obviously, a lot of people are afraid to undertake something new, yet there are plenty of examples of people "doing it." So, fear is not really the problem here. Rather we need to recognize how we hold fear in our lives. For example, do you treat fear as a challenge, something that energizes you and gets your adrenaline going? Do you face fear gingerly, approaching it slowly and carefully while you plan the next step? Or do you "freeze" up, refusing to explore the situation and possibly end up stagnating? These are important questions to ask yourself for becoming fully self-aware means developing the willingness to face fear and productively work through it. A starting point for doing this is to develop a healthy perspective of exactly what fear is. Susan Jeffers, in her book *Feel the Fear and Do It Anyway*, presents us with a clear, unthreatening way to accept fear in our lives in her "Five Truths About Fear:"

1. The fear will never go away as long as I continue to grow.

2. The only way to get rid of the fear of doing something is to go out...and do it.

3. The only way to feel better about myself is to go out...and do it.

4. Not only am I going to experience fear whenever I'm on unfamiliar territory, but so is everyone else.

5. Pushing through fear is less frightening than living with the underlying fear that comes from a feeling of helplessness.

Accepting that fear is a natural part of life will allow you to make "peace" with your fear. It can actually be a great asset for it can energize your feelings in a particular situation if you recognize how to use it. We recommend the following methods for converting fear into personal power. By using these techniques you reinforce positive self-esteem for you no longer allow yourself to be paralyzed by fear—you control it!

1. Recognize what you have control over and what you do not. We spend a large portion of our lives worrying about things we have no control over or problems that have not even occurred. Robert Frost put it well when he said, "The reason why worry kills more people than work is that more people worry than work.

2. Accept responsibility for your health, actions and the consequences of your behavior. When you stop casting blame on external forces and learn to hold yourself accountable for your choices, an inner strength will arise. You will feel freed from guilt and confusion.

3. Determine the payoffs you receive from letting fear immobilize you. How do you feel about yourself? What will be the positive outcomes of your situation based on your position? What will be the outcomes for any other people who are involved?

4. Determine the payoffs you will receive if you move beyond your fear. What are the personal outcomes and what are the outcomes for others. Compare these to the outcome of #3. What serves you best at this time?

5. Exercise choices. If you passively wait for others to give you what you desire in life, you may never receive it. You can choose a path that lets you experience love and self-esteem.

Fear is a deeply rooted human emotion. It is up to you as to whether you befriend it or fight it. A student recently wore a t-shirt with a saying on it that is a philosophy we could all adopt, "Don't sweat the small stuff . . . It's all small stuff.

TAKE RISKS

Moving beyond fear means being willing to take risks. This, in and of itself, can be "scary." Frank Farley, a psychologist at the University of Wisconsin, has made a career of studying risk takers and has found that there are some people who choose risky paths even when they don't have to. This person would be called a *Type T* personality. Farley says, "The classic Type T gets out there on the edge

They feel most fully alive the moment they plunge headlong into a frightening challenge. About one in four people is a Type T." These people seek the exhilaration of "living on the edge." It makes them feel fully alive.

Not all of us need to feel this intense sensation. We each have an optimal brain arousal level—the level at which we are the most comfortable with our mental alertness and activity. So we each seek enough stimulation to get this neuronal activity up to this comfortable level. It is important, therefore, to understand your own risk preference. If you are extremely uncomfortable with change and conflict, if you seek the familiar and the "known" then it would be unwise to jump into highly risky situations. You will most likely find yourself frozen in fear.

We do not recommend, however, that you avoid all risks. Change is a key to growth and growth is an outcome of self-awareness. There is a direct relationship between fear and risk taking—to embrace risk you have to be willing to face fear. Therefore, it is important to decide the kind and degree of risks you are willing to take so that you can maintain a sense of security and yet experience the stimulation of growth. Here are some recommendations for learning to be a risk taker:

1. **Be willing to experiment**. Expose yourself to new people who have made different choices in their lives. Consider new experiences such as taking a new class, or accepting a new job challenge.

2. **Be aware of when and how often you say "no" to new opportunities**. Practice taking new risks by saying "yes." Start by nodding your head and saying "yes" when you are alone. The physical head movement is very affirming in helping to create a new kinesthetic sense.

3. **Set realistic expectations.** Be sure the outcome of the risk is an attainable goal that is appropriate for you right now. Expecting too little of yourself is not a challenge. However, unrealistically high expectations can be discouraging.

"to be nobody—but yourself—in a world which is doing its best, night and day, to make you everybody else, means to fight the hardest battle which any human being can fight."   e.e. cummings

4. **Trust yourself**. Each time you take a risk and experience success, you will take huge steps in terms of your self-esteem. And your self-trust will grow.

5. **Trust others**. You cannot change another person's choices or behavior if he has not decided to change on his own. Deciding how much you are willing to trust another and with what, you slowly develop the intimacy of the relationship. Yes, it is a risk, but the payoff can be big!

6. **Do not force yourself to take a risk if you are not ready.** Do not say yes if you have great inner resistance. Learning to take risks is done step-by-step.

The world is filled with many "unknowns," including the ones that exist inside of each of us. Each time we take a risk we expand our role in the world. "Every time you acquire a new interest, even more, a new accomplishment, you increase your power of life," states William Lyon Phelps. And is not the **power** of life what "living" is all about?

FORGIVE YOURSELF

The heart of healthy self-esteem was pointed out when jazz great Eartha Kitt quipped,

> Yes, I'm my own best friend. I've always been that way, even when I felt other people didn't understand me, because I knew I still had to be true to myself. There were times when I allowed people to get me off the track about who I was but I'd analyze myself and find out what was happening before I got myself into something. I find that people who don't like themselves much are very difficult to be with. They are constantly searching to find out who they are, and therefore they are never very honest. It was the basic need for healthy survival that made me realize I had to be my own best friend.

Kitt seemed to know something many of us have forgotten and that is that self love is the very key of survival. Yet, loving oneself is often difficult in light of how hard we are on ourselves. We would like to recommend a way to clear the path to greater experiences in your life:

1. **Forgive yourself for not being "perfect."** The need to be perfect puts a lot of pressure on every situation you are in. You lose spontaneity and flexibility. You also resist learning from your mistakes because you will tend to obsess over the errors. Reward yourself for being human—take a walk in the park, go to a movie or get a massage. Treating yourself as a special and unique human worthy of positive experiences will lead to believing you are such a person!

2. **Make the best of what you are.** To live fully and productively make the best of your assets. Remember, you are **human**, and being human means occasionally having feelings you dislike. These are human feelings and the sooner you accept them, the sooner you will learn to appreciate your own uniqueness.

3. **Accept that you cannot please everyone.** Leo Buscaglia says "you can be the finest plum in the world. . . . But you must remember, there are people who do not like plums . . . You have the choice of becoming a banana. But you must be warned that if you choose to become a banana, you will be a second-rate banana. But you can always be the best plum."

4. **Participate in activities you enjoy.** Celebrate your creativity and strengths. Appreciate your inquisitive mind and use it in ways that give you pleasure. Doing something enjoyable will help you feel optimistic about your life.

5. **Appreciate your body.** Taking time to attend to your physical well-being will give you one less area to criticize—and this is an important self-esteem subject for most of us. Being responsible means caring for yourself as well as others.

6. **Live with integrity.** Taking responsibility for your actions without blaming others or acting like a victim requires a very important choice. That choice is to live honestly and with integrity. Being honest with others demands being honest with yourself. It takes courage to "own" our actions, to be sensitive to others and to live in a tolerant and nurturing way.

Forgiving yourself is the greatest gift you can give, not only to yourself but to those you share your life with. For, when you release the negative thoughts and stop punishing yourself for the past or for things you do not control, you step into the exciting territory of greater self exploration. We saw this when one of our students made this major step. Marty, a woman with a history of childhood sexual abuse, felt she was an unworthy victim of life. She found herself caught in a dangerous cycle of obsessive eating behaviors that were having severe effects on her physical and emotional health. To make matters worse, she constantly found herself in painful arguments with those she loved which simply led her to believe that she was a bad influence and an unworthy person. She often considered suicide and, more than once, was almost hospitalized for erratic behavior. Not knowing where to turn she slowly began a process of self-searching and when she finally started to acknowledge that she was not perfect, she began to forgive herself of her "human" flaws. At this point a miracle occurred—she relaxed!! She smiled more often, felt more in control of her behavior and began to deal with her life in the present. She found she could actually express love to those in her life. She was back on track!

Marty struggled for years before she came to the realization that she had worth. When we deal with our fears and let go of our resentment toward ourselves and others, like Marty, we can begin to live productively in the present. As Oscar Wilde said, "To love oneself is the beginning of a lifelong romance."

FORGIVE OTHERS

The moment you let go of your resentment of the people you feel have hurt or betrayed you, you can begin to heal emotional wounds that have kept high self esteem blocked. Carrying hostility around requires a tremendous amount of energy and depletes your ability to live constructively in the "present." It is also important to accept forgiveness from others. When there is mutual agreement with another person to let go of the past you give up the burden of guilt. This will allow you to move on with your life.

We can be instrumental in helping to nurture self-esteem and self-worth in others when we let go of our emotional wounds. Marianne Williamson, in her book *A Return to Love,* states, "In every relationship, in every moment, we teach either love or fear. To teach is to demonstrate. As we demonstrate love towards others we learn that we are lovable and we learn to love more deeply."

Out of the research presented by the California Task Force on Self-Esteem have come the following recommendations to truly be role models of self-worth and love.

1. **Give personal attention.** Be willing to listen with an open mind and an open heart.

2. **Demonstrate respect, acceptance and support.** "The only justification we have to look down on someone is because we are about to pick him up." When Jesse Jackson made this statement he pointed to a key in healthy relationships. We begin to feel we are worthy when others show us respect. Don't get caught in the manipulative idea that someone must "earn" your respect. The more freely and supportively you give it, the more you help others believe they are worth it!

3. **Encourage healthy achievement.** As long as the expectations you communicate to others are realistic, then you help others see that they can stretch their limits and become more then they are *right now.*

4. **Provide a sensible structure.** Be fair and consistent as you develop and apply structure in your relationships. People need a certain amount of predictability to feel secure.

[handwritten] Slavery / seaming

5. **Appreciate the benefits of a multicultural society.** "Variety is the spice of life" is certainly true in the course of human relationships. Celebrate the richness and diversity other people offer you. Life would be so boring if we were all the same!

6. **Negotiate Conflicts.** Respecting the dignity of another human being means **not inflicting** shame, injury or pain. Such things only reveal the "weakness" of the doer.

7. **Encourage autonomy and competence**. You accept your role as a "human being" when you encourage others to be risk takers and to meet challenges. You like yourself better when you can also celebrate others' successes. As Martin Walsh says, "When you look for the good in others you discover the best in yourself"

It has often been said that there are two basic emotions from which all others stem. Those emotions are love and fear. Growth occurs when you take a risk and face your fears, both the fears within you and the fears that involve others. The sense of accomplishment you experience at this point will lead you to the realization that a healthy self-concept has been alive and within you all the time.

At this point love can become real in your life. Love is your birthright—love of self and of others. Embracing this basic emotion can be your most important step in becoming fully human. Mother Teresa, one the greatest advocates for loving and caring, encourages you by saying "If we want a love message to be heard, it has got to be sent out. To keep a lamp burning, we have to keep putting oil in it." So, pour "oil" into those who need it most! The more freely you pour love into yourself and others, the more it will open doors to your greatest fulfillment.

IN CONCLUSION

This book has been our way of sharing what is our passion as professionals, as well as our life-long personal search. The realm of human potential is truly a great frontier, filled with exciting adventures and valuable discoveries and we hope you will use the tools presented here to help you become a committed and successful explorer. This book is our gift to you. Your gift to us is that, at the end of your own journey, you not only have increased your self-awareness but, more importantly, have learned how to love yourself as a unique and valuable member of humanity. We leave you with these last words and wish you luck on your journey:

"One young man was asked by a solicitous questioner what he could do better than anyone else. It was the assumption of the person who asked the question that everyone has some attribute at which he excels. Thus the question was intended to help the young man discover this attribute in order to increase his self-esteem. But the answer that the questioner received was one that he was probably not prepared for. For the young man, who seemed very comfortable and self-assured, replied, "I can be **me** better then anyone else in the world."

This is the real answer to the question. Each one of us can be the unique individual self that we are, better than anyone else. And it is impossible to compare such individuals because it is like comparing apples and oranges. *We are all best at being different and unique......."*

Lou Benson

UNIT THREE
Activities for Self-Discovery

SECTION ONE

Exercises For Exploring the

Self-Concept
Self-Image
Self-Esteem

WHO AM I?

Part One: Answer the question *Who Am I?* by listing the characteristics that you feel distinguish you from others. You can include adjectives that describe your personal qualities, roles you play or beliefs you have about yourself. Your list could include words such as *determined, sister, stubborn, mechanic, caring, hardworking, uncertain,* and so on.

1. Challenging
2. Clean
3. uncertain
4. Daring
5. Deep
6. stubborn
7. Modern
8. Dreamy
9. Sensitive
10. Creative
11. Artistic
12. Dishonest
13. emotional
14. Fashionable
15. insightful
16. Impatient
17. Impulsive
18. Forgetful
19. Mess
20. Careless

What were your answers centered around? (For example, roles, physical attributes, talents, etc.)

What beliefs are reflected in your answers?

What do your answers tell you about your positive/negative self views?

(✓)

Part Two: Go back to your original list and prioritize it, with number one being the descriptor that is most important and number twenty being the descriptor that is least important to you:

1. Artistic

2. Fashionable

3. Insightful

4. Sensitive

5. Emotional

6. Deep

7. Daring

8. Challenging

9. Creative

10. Forgetful

11. Careless

12. Stubborn

13. Modern

14. Dishonest

15. Impatian

16. Impulsive

17. Dreamy!

18. Clean

19. Mess

20. uncertain

With your eyes closed, imagine yourself without each of the qualities on the list, starting with the one on the bottom. How important is each quality to your total view of self?

Which of these qualities make you feel good about yourself?

Artistic, Fashionable, Insightful, Sensitive, Emotional, Daring, Challenging, Creative, Deep, Modern

Which of these qualities make you feel more negative?

Uncertain, Mess, Careless, Forgetful, Dreamy, Impatient, Impulsive, Dishonest

o <u>modesty</u> (n) (quiet success) the quality of not talking about or not trying to make people notice your abilities and achievements.

Jan. 20. 2019

UNDERSTANDING MY SELF-CONCEPT

During the course of a day we often focus on what we have communicated positively or negatively to others. Understanding that those thoughts are reflections of our self-concept can help us understand our communication patterns better

The purpose of this activity is to examine what you feel are your strengths as a communicator and the areas you feel have been barriers to your own personal success. Focus on your personal qualities that have strengthened your communication ability. We are asking you to be realistic and honest. There is no room for <u>modesty</u> here. By increasing your self-awareness you increase your self-acceptance. Give the same attention to the areas you would like to improve upon.

Part I: List the six characteristics that you feel have increased your abilities as a communicator and the six that may distract your effectiveness:

MY STRENGTHS

1. Positive Thinkers

2. Friendly

3. Empathy

4. Confident

5. Observing

MY WEAKNESSES

1. Bragging about myself

2. Constantly interrupting

3. Equating my experience

4. It's all about me

5. Reading others's mind

Unit Three: Activities For Self-Discovery

Part II: Complete the following statements:

1. My positive accomplishments/successes are:

- I have made good friend "Joey & " Chris "

2. The strengths I use to achieve success are:

- confident, positive thinker, Friendly

blockade
rào chắn   sử dụng

3. The barriers to utilizing my strengths are:
(How to use ur strengths to overcome my weaknesses)

4. The self-concept I would like to change the most is:
" It's all about me" and "bragging "

Explain: I always feel my problem is more important than everyone and I want to get other's attention.
I also want people know that I am happy and I have friends. I brag about myself.

5. My goals to develop/maintain a positive self-concept are:
- I have power to change myself
- I am a great artistic
- I am a brilliant and creative artist
- I am unique, kind, brave and strong

6. The specific steps I will take to develop/maintain a positive self-concept are

1 Study myself
2 Heal
3 Take Risk
4 Do things I love
5 Beg Commitment w/ myself
6 Be bestfriend with myself

WHAT IS MY SELF-IMAGE?

PURPOSE: To help you discover the components of the mental image you hold of yourself.

thành lập

ANSWER THE FOLLOWING QUESTIONS:

1. How do I act around:

    My family: Ignorance, anger, unrespecful, Yelling, screaming, cussing, stop talking to Dad and brother many years

    My friends: Friendly, kind, caring, open mind, positive. "I would things make you happy"

    My fellow employees/boss: Friendly, team-player, affraid, shy, being funny, sometime respect, sometimes not respect. Try to get their attention

2. How do others react to me:

    My family: Unkind, My dad doesn't care. My brother said "đồ ăn bám", My aunt said "con kó nuôi mẹ đc, it ký" My mom has no respect for me.

    My friends: I only have Joey who honestly Love me. - Brandi respect me. Other friends look down on me when they see my weakness (Neoh, Dahye). they are fake to me.

    My fellow employees/boss:
    - We are friendly to each other and respect each other.

119

3. How does my nonverbal communication (dress, body language, etc.) affect those around me?

   - The way dress (elegant, clean) draw attention to other
   - My friendly approaching (bending my head when say hi) gave a bright wide smile) create a jordy talking environm
   - My face expression shows empathy and kindness to others

4. How does the reaction of others toward me affect my self-image?

   My family: Yelling at me, bullied me, use mean words when talked w/ me " ngu như cức, làm biến, ăn bám ít kỹ , ..."

   My friends: Neoh " đại gái, em ko đi đẹp thì em phải nên hiền

   My fellow employees/boss:
   Thinking I am stupid but still respecting me
   They thought I barely know anything

5. If I could change something about my self-image, it would be:

   - Seem stupid to my co-workers
   - Unrespect / dramaaa
   - Moody
   - Not being calm
   - Bragging

DO I LIKE ME?

Understanding our self-concept often leads to exploring feelings of self-approval or disapproval. The following test is designed to help you determine how happy you are with yourself. Use the scale as follows:

1	NEVER
2	RARELY
3	SOMETIMES
4	USUALLY
5	ALWAYS

1. __3__ Most people like me.

2. __5__ I like how my body looks.

3. __4__ I enjoy my work.

4. __4__ I'm comfortable around strangers.

5. __5__ I enjoy new experiences.

6. __2__ I like getting up in the morning.

7. __3__ I express how I feel.

8. __2__ I have valuable opinions.

9. __3__ I'm a special person.

10. __2__ I feel in control of my life.

11. __5__ I know what my goals are.

12. __3__ Other people care about me.

13. __4__ I deserve good things in life.

14. __5__ I enjoy my spare time.

15. __5__ I have a lot to look forward to.

16. __4__ I'm an interesting person.

17. __1__ I enjoy my relationships.

18. __5__ I am an optimist.

19. __4__ I'm an attractive person.

20. __1__ I can laugh at my mistakes.

21. __5__ There's little I'm ashamed of.

22. __3__ I enjoy my home.

23. __3__ I respect myself.

24. __4__ I enjoy each day.

QUESTIONS FOR SELF-EXPLORATION

Answer the following questions openly and honestly:

1. Write four words that describe you:
   - Brave
   - Emotional
   - Bragging
   - Impulsive

2. Describe your personality by writing 5 sentences about yourself:
   - I am easy going
   - I love to crack joke
   - I am quiet in a group of people
   - I have no judgment for anyone
   - I always try to do anything could help myself grow

3. List three goals you have for personal improvement:

   - Become more proactive
   - Become more mindful
   - Build relationship with myself
   - Read more. Read often
   - Communication
   - Work on my growth mindset.
   - Increase my willpower.
   - Stop Procastinating
   - Wake up early

4. Select a color, an animal, an object and a flower that describes you:
   - white
   - Wolf
   - Camera
   - Daisy

• <u>Formative</u> (adj) (thành lập) relating to the time when someone or sth is starting to develop in character.

Unit Three: Activities For Self-Discovery

5. What do you worry about most?

    Not able to find my truth-self & have my own interest.

6. Write about a major event that was pleasant:

    - Sitting in the theater
    - Doing dance concert
    - Work on my art in the studios

7. Write about a major event that was sad:

    - Seperating with Esther.
    - Seeing my mom broken down because of my dad
    - Seeing my little crying because she got yelled at

8. Write about your most embarrassing moment:

    - Stole stuff from my classmate
    - Sexually approached my classmate when 5 years old & 15 years old
    - Sucking my thumb until high school
    - Pulling my hair until college

9. Write about an incident from your childhood that was deeply <u>formative</u>:

    - Sexually violated
    - Bullied

10. Write about a personal secret:

    - Got bullied
    - Sexually abuse

124

Exercises For Exploring the Self-Concept, Self-Image and Self-Esteem

11. What currently frustrates you the most?

    - My own passion (Art). I feel I am not putting my time into it.

12. What is your most serious problem?

    - Healing myself - I need to be creative

13. What gives you the greatest joy?

    - Drawing, being creative . taking pictures, editing images Traveling, Panting, clothes . reading.

14. Write about a peak experience in your life:

15. Have you ever had a mystical experience? If so, please describe:

16. Describe your relationship with your father:

    Worse   Havn't talk in years

    I hate him

17. Describe your relationship with your mother:

     I love her but she barely understand me

18. Describe your relationship with your siblings:

     - I hate my brother

     - I love my little sister very much. she shares everything she has with me

19. Describe your relationship with your "significant other" (boy/girlfriend, spouse, etc.)

     - I always have Problem w/ my friends

20. Describe your relationship with yourself:

     - I try to understand myself - love myself -

     - I'm not really know myself

COLLAGE EXPERIENCE

This activity is designed to provide an experience in self-disclosure. It will also allow others to understand your self-concept better.

Procedure: Construct a collage which represents the **real you**: Consider the following when creating it:

Design:

1. The shape, color and design.

2. The story it tells about you.

3. The blank spaces or sense of "fullness"

4. The materials you use:

    Be creative—use magazine photos, souvenirs, personal objects and pictures, words, shapes, etc.

5. It may be a poster, a box showing your inside/outside self, a mobile or any other creative representation of "you."

Content:

1. Your collage must have a minimum of 10 items and a maximum of 20 about self.

2. It must include at least 5 secrets or privileged information that you don't normally reveal about yourself when first meeting someone.

3. The following are possible areas to cover:

How do you see yourself? How do you see your family?

The place where you feel most at home.

Your strong points.

People (no more than 3) most important to you.

What are your fears?

What makes you angry?

What would you like to change about yourself?

What life crises have occurred in your life?

Things you like best to do (no more than 2).

What would you do if you had one year left to live?

If you could be an animal, what would you choose and why?

The event/person that caused your greatest joy.

The event/person that caused your greatest pain.

Presentation:

The presentation is an opportunity for us to understand the "real you." This is more than a "get acquainted" time. Self-disclosure leads to more authentic relationships! People will be allowed to ask you follow-up questions.

WHERE AM I NOW?

We find ourselves in a large number of situations in life in which we play a variety of roles. Identifying our self-concept can help us understand our reactions. For each category list five of your personal characteristics in order of importance (starting with the most important in your life):

1. Describe your physical condition (the condition of your body):

    Good - but I want to get stronger

2. Describe the social characteristics that you communicate to others: (friendly, cool...)

    Friendly . I got really quiet in a group of people or at the party.

3. Describe your mental abilities:

4. List the "moods" best describe you:

    - Anger
    - Sad
    - Mad
    - Hurt
    - Insecure
    - Confused
    - critical
    - Frustrated
    -

5. List the "beliefs" that best describe you (i.e. spiritual, activist, conservative, etc.)

   - Committing to courage · Embodying honesty
   - kindness
   - Love
   - Taking Risk & learning from mistake

6. Describe those things that make you proud:

   - Camera, taking photo
   - Art ; Painting, drawing
   - studying myself

7. Describe those things that disappoint you:

   - Not trying hard
   -

8. Describe your talents:

9. Describe those things that you enjoy sharing with others:

10. Describe those things that you choose to keep to yourself:

HOW SENSITIVE ARE YOU?

The following questionnaire has been designed to help you realize sensitivity determines how a person will perceive and communicate. Using the scale below, individually answer the Self-Report Device.

SENSITIVITY SELF-REPORT DEVICE

Rating Scale:

1—Very highly sensitive to; very important; could change your actions

2—Sensitive to; matters but won't impede action; may modify

3—Aware of; will take into consideration; but will not let it affect actions at all

4—Not very aware of; don't really pay much attention to; of little importance

5—Not aware of; does not matter one way or the other

SELF:

How Sensitive Are You Toward	Circle Appropriate Response				
1. Your appearance	1	2	3	4	5
2. Your mental attitude	1	2	3	4	5
3. Tension	1	2	3	4	5
4. Your physical health	1	2	3	4	5
5. Bodily symptoms	1	2	3	4	5
6. Your creativity and assets	1	2	3	4	5
7. Your awareness	1	2	3	4	5
8. Alertness	1	2	3	4	5

		1	2	3	4	5
9.	Motivation	1	2	3	4	5
10.	Fatigue	1	2	3	4	5
11.	Your failures	1	2	3	4	5
12.	Your successes	1	2	3	4	5
13.	Your fears	1	2	3	4	5
14.	Your personal problems	1	2	3	4	5
15.	Decisions you must make	1	2	3	4	5
16.	Your opinions of others	1	2	3	4	5
17.	Your behavior towards others	1	2	3	4	5
18.	Your verbal communication	1	2	3	4	5
19.	Your body language	1	2	3	4	5
20.	Your shortcomings	1	2	3	4	5
21.	Personality	1	2	3	4	5
22.	Handicaps	1	2	3	4	5
23.	Position and status	1	2	3	4	5
24.	Interpersonal competition	1	2	3	4	5
25.	Aptitude	1	2	3	4	5

Other People:

		1	2	3	4	5
1.	Your family's problems	1	2	3	4	5
2.	Your spouse's feelings and needs	1	2	3	4	5
3.	Your job requirements	1	2	3	4	5
4.	Fellow employees' opinions of you	1	2	3	4	5
5.	Criticism of you	1	2	3	4	5

6.	Criticism of things you do	1	2	3	4	5
7.	Society's ills	1	2	3	4	5
8.	Mass Movement	1	2	3	4	5
9.	Fads	1	2	3	4	5
10.	Smoking	1	2	3	4	5
11.	Drinking	1	2	3	4	5
12.	Obnoxious behavior	1	2	3	4	5
13.	Changes in plans	1	2	3	4	5
14.	Appearance	1	2	3	4	5
15.	Personality	1	2	3	4	5
16.	Strong points (assets)	1	2	3	4	5
17.	Shortcomings	1	2	3	4	5
18.	Handicaps	1	2	3	4	5
19.	Educational level	1	2	3	4	5
20.	Position and status	1	2	3	4	5
21.	Achievement	1	2	3	4	5
22.	Competing with you	1	2	3	4	5
23.	Judgment of you	1	2	3	4	5
24.	Compliments of you	1	2	3	4	5
25.	Advice to you	1	2	3	4	5

Other Variables:

1.	Parties	1	2	3	4	5
2.	Politics	1	2	3	4	5
3.	Environment	1	2	3	4	5

Unit Three: Activities For Self-Discovery

4.	Money issues	1	2	3	4	5
5.	The weather	1	2	3	4	5
6.	The sunshine	1	2	3	4	5
7.	Crowded places	1	2	3	4	5
8.	Arguments	1	2	3	4	5
9.	Meetings	1	2	3	4	5
10.	School counselors	1	2	3	4	5
11.	Colors	1	2	3	4	5
12.	Smells	1	2	3	4	5
13.	Visual stimulation	1	2	3	4	5
14.	Smog	1	2	3	4	5
15.	Disappointment	1	2	3	4	5
16.	Change of plans	1	2	3	4	5
17.	The media	1	2	3	4	5
18.	Poverty	1	2	3	4	5
19.	Art forms	1	2	3	4	5
20.	Religion	1	2	3	4	5
21.	Music	1	2	3	4	5
22.	Death	1	2	3	4	5
23.	Sex	1	2	3	4	5
24.	Television	1	2	3	4	5
25.	Newspapers	1	2	3	4	5

SCORING:

1. Add your scores for each of the three areas. The area in which you earn the lowest score is the area in which you are the most sensitive.

2. Based on the activity place a "yes" or "not" next to the following statements:

   _____ I am very aware of myself.

   _____ I am sensitive to others.

   _____ I need positive reinforcement from others.

   _____ Other's opinions of me really makes a difference.

   _____ I don't care what others think of me, but I am sensitive to their needs and how I might help them.

   _____ I am basically an individualist.

3. Answer the following questions:

   a. Are you basically a "sensitive" person?

   b. Are you more sensitive to yourself or to others?

   c. What part does perception play in sensitivity?

    d. Do you see any way in which you are hindered by your sensitivity?

    e. How does your sensitivity help you?

    f. Is there any area you'd like to increase your sensitivity in?

GETTING TO KNOW ME

Complete the following statements:

1. I like...

2. I'm afraid of...

3. Children...

4. I hate...

5. I wish...

6. My life...

7. When he/she says something I don't like, I...

8. Others annoy me when...

9. Marriage...

10. My ambition is...

11. I most regret...

12. I consider myself...

13. When I make a mistake, I...

14. My greatest weakness is...

15. I think of myself as...

16. When things go against me, I...

17. I usually get nervous when...

18. My friends think that I...

19. My greatest joy...

20. Few people know that I...

HOW CONFIDENT AM I?

Understanding how confident we are in different situations, roles and with different people can give us insight into "who" we are. Rate your level of confidence on the following scale:

1 – I feel paralyzed by my fear of failure
2 – I feel very self conscious and fearful
3 – I feel somewhat inferior but am willing to try
4 – I still feel uncertain but feel I have some chance for success
5 – I feel very confident and will be successful

1. _____ With my physical body

2. _____ In my relationship with my parents

3. _____ In my relationship with my siblings

4. _____ With people I find attractive

5. _____ In front of a group

6. _____ As an employee

7. _____ In a leadership position

8. _____ In an interview

9. _____ In athletic activities

10. _____ Taking on a big project

11. _____ In my academic abilities

12. _____ In a conflict situation with strangers

13. _____   In a conflict situation with someone I'm having a relationship with

14. _____   Taking a chance on something I've never tried

15. _____   In my ability as a communicator

16. _____   As a friend

17. _____   With my creative or artistic abilities

18. _____   When traveling in unknown locations

19. _____   In trusting others

20. _____   In liking who I am

Answer the following questions:

1. What areas of your life do you feel the most confident in? Why?

2. What areas of your life do you feel the least confident in? Why?

3. How does your self-confidence affect the way you communicate with others?

"I CAN TAKE A COMPLIMENT!"

PURPOSE: To learn how to accept compliments, while at the same time acknowledging your assets.

Part One: In the space below, write down 15 qualities you like best about yourself. These may include talents, physical, emotional or mental characteristics, values, etc.

1.

2.

3.

4.

5.

6.

7.

8.

9.

10.

11.

12.

13.

14.

15.

Unit Three: Activities For Self-Discovery

Part Two: In either a group of classmates or close friends, sit quietly and listen while each person tells you what he/she admires the most about you. YOU CANNOT **DISCOUNT** (verbally or nonverbally) ANYTHING THAT IS SAID. You may thank individuals for the compliments. In the space below write down the things people told you:

Part Three: Answer the following questions:

1. How do the qualities you wrote about yourself compare to the qualities others complimented you on?

2. How did you feel while receiving the compliments?

3. How do you feel about your self-image now?

SECTION TWO

Exercises For Developing
Your Internal Processes

OWNING MY SEMANTICS

For the next week you will be asked to create an awareness of your language choices. The goal is to realign your language to help you create a more positive self view.

Procedure:

1. You will log the results of five situations in which you used semantic realignment.

2. Identify the situation and the person/people involve.

3. Describe what you were saying that was not positive in nature.

4. Describe the reaction(s).

5. Describe the language change you made to try and achieve a positive outcome.

6. Describe the reaction(s).

Log 1

Situation/Person:

Your Behavior (negative):

Reaction:

Your language change:

Reaction:

Log 2

Situation/Person:

Your Behavior (negative):

Reaction:

Your language change:

Reaction:

Log 3

Situation/Person:

Your Behavior (negative):

Reaction:

Your language change:

Reaction:

Log 4

Situation/Person:

Your Behavior (negative):

Reaction:

Your language change:

Reaction:

Log 5

Situation/Person:

Your Behavior (negative):

Reaction:

Your language change:

Reaction:

Unit Three: Activities for Self-Discovery

Answer the following discussion questions:

1. How did you feel when using semantic realignment?

2. What feedback did you receive from others about this change?

3. Are you going to continue using the language changes? Why or why not?

SELF-TALK FOR CHANGE

The following activity is designed to help you practice creating and using affirmations. Remember, the five elements of an effective affirmation are:

Personal, Positive, Present Tense, Emotional and Visual

Procedure: You will select:

1. Four goals that are achievable in the next six weeks.

2. For each goal, write in the space below 4 positive affirmations outlining your plan of action.

   FOR EXAMPLE:
   Goal: To lose 15 pounds
   Affirmations:
   - I am my desired weight of 135 lbs..
   - I enjoy eating fresh vegetables and drinking lots of water.
   - I enjoy exercising at the gym every other day.
   - I am happy and confident in my body at 135 lbs., size ten, trim and fit.

1. **Goal:**

   Affirmations:

Unit Three: Activities for Self-Discovery

2. **Goal:**

   Affirmations:

3. **Goal:**

   Affirmations:

4. **Goal:**

   Affirmations:

THE AWAKENING OF A SLEEPING GIANT

Mental Literacy may be described as the King of Literacies. We pour hundreds of billions of dollars worldwide into completing our mastery of verbal, numerical and other forms of literacy, while ignoring the most basic and most important "alphabet" of all—the alphabet of the brain.

Possessing this one fundamental literacy, we will be able to master the others with ease. Most of you who are reading this article will be both literate and numerate. To give you a good guide to your current MLQ (Mental Literacy Quotient) consider the following:

In your entire school career, were you taught more than two hours about:

		YES	NO
1.	The number of your brain cells and how they function?	_____	_____
2.	The difference in your memory functions *while* you learn and *after* you have learned?	_____	_____
3.	How to apply your creativity to any subject?	_____	_____
4.	How the way your thinking affects the growth of your brain cells?	_____	_____
5.	How to "ride the waves" of concentration?	_____	_____
6.	How to raise your I.Q.?	_____	_____
7.	The relationship between physical and mental health?	_____	_____
8.	How to apply learning theory to your *own* learning?	_____	_____
9.	The different functions of your left and right cortex?	_____	_____
10.	The rhythms of memory?	_____	_____

151

11. Your eye/brain relationship and how to control them for improving the taking in of information?   _____ _____

12. How to take notes that increase both your memory *and* your creativity?   _____ _____

DO YOU THINK:

13. Memory naturally declines with age?   _____ _____

14. The brain looses brain cells with age?   _____ _____

15. Children learn languages faster than adults?   _____ _____

16. Each alcoholic drink costs you 1,000 brain cells?   _____ _____

HAVE YOU EVER CAUGHT YOURSELF SAYING THINGS LIKE:

17. I'm not creative.   _____ _____

18. I have the world's worst memory.   _____ _____

19. I'm not very good at math.   _____ _____

20. I can't sing.   _____ _____

21. I can't do art.   _____ _____

22. I'm stupid.   _____ _____

CIRCLE THE CORRECT ANSWER:

23. The percentage of the brain we consciously use is:

A. 50%   B. 20%   C. 1%

CREATIVITY EXERCISE:

24.   A. In one minute, jot down all the possible uses you can think of for a paper clip.

          B. Next, do exactly the same, this time jotting down all those things which you *can not* use a paper clip.

You would be truly Mentally Literate if you answered all the first 12 questions with a "yes," questions 13-22 with a "no," the percentage of brain use with 1%, the positive paper clip uses with eight or more in a minute, and the negative uses with zero! A score of even 30% on these questions would place you in the top one percent of the Mentally Literate.

Why *do* we have this enormous lack of knowledge about that sleeping giant we all carry with us every second of our lives? Because the science of our brain is truly in its infancy. 95% of what we now know about the human brain has been discovered in the last ten years. The brain itself has only existed in its present form for some 45 thousand years—a mere twinkling of an eye in the context of evolutionary history. And it is only in the last five hundred years that scientists have come to recognize that our mental skills are located in our heads. Not surprisingly, we are still experiencing teething problems as we take our first tottering steps to discover how our brains work and how to use them.

Reprinted by permission, Tony Buzan, President, The Brain Foundation and founder of the Brain Trust.

153

EXPERIENCING THE HEMISPHERES

This activity will allow you to experience the different ways in which your two hemispheres process information.

PROCEDURE:

PART ONE:

1. Find a comfortable place to sit (do not lay down.)

2. Close your eyes and **relax** your body.

3. Focus on your breathing, feeling yourself relax with every inhale. Feel yourself **let go** of tension with every exhale. Do this for at least seven breaths.

PART TWO:

1. In this relaxed state, direct your eyes into your left brain.

2. Imagine a light being turned on in the room of your left brain.

3. Look around and see what is there. Notice the details.

4. Now, direct your eyes into your right brain and repeat the same steps. Notice the details in this hemisphere.

5. There should be distinct differences between what you notice in each room. Make a mental note of these differences.

PART THREE:

1. Return your attention (eyes closed) to the left brain. Imagine the letter "A" in this room.

2. Now shift your attention to the right brain and imagine the letter "B" in this room.

3. Go back to the left brain and imagine the letter "C."

4. Shift again to the right brain and imagine the letter "D."

5. Continue shifting back and forth between each hemisphere as you imagine every letter of the alphabet.

PART FOUR:

1. Continue shifting between the hemispheres, only now imagine different objects of different colors. For example: LEFT–"Red Ball," and RIGHT–"Green Triangle," and so on.

2. You can continue this process by imagining any variety of objects, animals, food, scenes, and so on. The purpose is to continue to notice the differences as you shift attention between hemispheres.

PART FIVE:

1. Bring your attention into the left brain and imagine the first half of a figure eight.

2. As you complete this first circle, continue following it into the right brain.

3. You will carry this line across the middle of the brain, drawing the circle through the right brain, back to the middle of the brain and on into the left brain again.

4. Continue making this figure eight, back and forth across the hemispheres.

5. Feel the sensations as you link up the two hemispheres.

6. Make at least 12 Figure Eights.

REACTIONS:

1. What physical sensations did you notice during this exercise?

2. What were the differences in the images as you switched from side to side?

3. Did you find one side easier than the other to access? If so, which one and why do you believe this happened?

4. What changes occurred when you were using the Figure Eight (physical, imagery, sensory, etc...?)

SUPER-LEARNING VISUALIZATION

This activity is designed to help you understand your potential by exploring the greater capabilities of your brain.

Procedure:

1. Find yourself a comfortable spot, sit or lie down, close your eyes and relax

2. Begin to focus on your breathing patterns. With every inhale think "RELAX." With every exhale think "LET GO."

3. When the body is deeply relaxed, you can enter the domain of the "mind's eye" where whatever you vividly see, hear, feel, taste, or smell becomes reality for the brain and the nervous system.

4. Visualize the following sequence of events, feelings and sensory experiences. (You can pre-record this in your own voice if you do not want to simply "play" it on your own.)

Visualization:

In your "mind's eye," see yourself walking along a pathway. The sun is brightly shining above and there are soft, white, puffy clouds in the skies. The bird's are singing as they soar through the skies. You feel comfortable and at peace with yourself and with the world about you. Look around and see what trees, flowers or scenery surround this very peaceful path you are walking on. Remember to see the scenery in vivid color and detail.

While you are walking along this pathway, think about yourself as a student. Gently allow all the many positives that you possess as a student flow through your mind. As you allow your many positives to flow through your awareness, you become aware of four attributes that if you added these to your repertoire of abilities you could become an even better student—a SUPER STUDENT." Perhaps they may be increased self-discipline, increased self-confidence, math abilities, better recall, greater comprehension, whatever you could possibly need.

Make the mental decision that, if you found a way to incorporate these desired abilities within you, you would make the commitment to do so. As you make this commitment, ahead on the right hand side of your path, see a big red schoolhouse. See the steeple on the top and hear the schoolbells ringing a welcome for you. As you approach the schoolhouse, you feel the enthusiasm and joy of learning that a four-year old child has. You recall when learning was **fun and easy** for you!

Place your hand on the door knob and enter the schoolhouse. Inside you see a brightly lit and cheerful classroom. On the shelves that surround the classroom are beautiful glass containers with colorful crystallized sugar inside them. Written on the outside of each glass container is a word. For example, on one you see, **Joy of Learning,** on another you see good study skills, or perfect recall, the ability to easily memorize.

As you are reading all the labels, you are approached by a teacher. You know this person is a master teacher, one who inspires their students and is fun to learn from. As he or she smiles at you, hear this teacher tell you that you have found your way to the MAGICAL SCHOOLHOUSE. Because you have found your way here, you may choose any four of the glass containers that line the shelves of the schoolroom. He or she can then blend them into an ELIXIR OF CHANGE for you to drink. Give yourself sufficient time to choose from all of the learning capabilities. Make your favorite four choices and take them with you to the teacher's desk. Watch as the teacher takes the four glass containers and pours the multi-colored sugar crystals into a blender on the desk. Watch as crushed ice is added into the blender and turned on. See the swirling kaleidoscope of colors blending together. Within this elixir are the desired ingredients for change which you chose from the shelves. Watch as the master teacher pours the elixir of change into a goblet and hands it to you.

If you truly desire these qualities within you then slowly sip the savory liquid. This elixir has a fragrant taste that is especially pleasing to you. Focus on that taste so you fully anchor it in your memory. Feel the coolness of the liquid as it slowly moves across your lips . . . across your tongue . . . down your throat and into your stomach for digestion. Carefully sip every drop of the elixir and follow the sensations as the liquid makes its journey from the glass to the lips and down through the throat to the stomach. As all of the elixir is now in your stomach, shift all of your attention here and feel the sensations of energy begin to circulate as the stomach juices slowly digest all the ingredients of change in you.

Now feel the electricity begin to slowly move throughout your entire nervous system as the blood begins to distribute all the ingredients for change throughout your entire body. You will probably feel tingling sensations, heat or cold as the ingredients move throughout the various parts of your body. Feel a total shift in the body as the ingredients move into your brain and become a total catalyst for change. Know and feel that these four qualities are now within you waiting to be actualized by your external behaviors. You are surprised, but excited by how easily change can occur when you imagine it.

Now express your appreciation to the master teacher for combining the elixir. Hear this person tell you that you can return at any time that you choose to add in other qualities or to refresh the ones you chose today. After thanking the master teacher, turn again towards the door to the schoolhouse and open the door. Walk outside into the bright sunlight, walking back up the pathway, you feel the lightness of your step, the enthusiasm in your body for learning and you know for certain that you will be able to fully actualize all of these new capabilities and become the Super Student you have desired to be.

When you are ready to return from your waking daydream. See a puffy white cloud of light standing on your pathway. See yourself walking into the cloud of light and then you begin to increase the depth of your breathing. Breath at least seven times, mentally telling yourself to re-energize with each deep inhale and to revitalize with each exhale. Slowly stretch your muscles back to an alert state before you open your eyes.

When you are alert again, sit up with a smile on your lips, and welcome back, better and more capable than ever.

A MEDITATION BREAK

Relaxation techniques have been found to boost the immune system, reduce stress and increase a sense of "long-term" tranquility in your life. Use the following technique and you can enjoy the benefits of relaxation and meditation everyday!

Location: Find a quiet place free from distractions. You may want to use a blanket or extra clothing as you may get chilled as you relax due to the natural drop in your metabolic rate.

Method:

1. Sit erect or lay flat. It is important that your spine is straight and that your neck and shoulders are relaxed and in a straight line with your spine.

2. If sitting, keep feet flat on the floor. If laying down, do not cross feet.

3. Keep your hands relaxed, palms up.

4. Take several deep breaths through your nose. Keep eyes closed.

5. Starting at the toes scan your body for any tension. If you find any, tell that part of your body to relax.

6. Focus on your breath. If your mind wanders, simply observe the thoughts and bring your attention back to your breath.

7. To help you keep focused on your breath say the following words to yourself as you breathe in and out. Spend several minutes on each pair before moving on:

IN BREATH	OUT BREATH
In	Out
Relax	Release
Let	Go
Calm	Peace
Joy	Love

8. Change the words if there are others that will be more productive to you.

9. When you have achieved a sense of total relaxation slowly bring your attention back to your body. Scan your body starting at the toes and moving upward, until you feel connected and alert.

10. Make a commitment to take this sense of relaxation with you throughout the day. It can help you to stay centered and calm in many situations.

UNDERSTANDING HOW MY BODY FEELS

Expressing our innermost feelings can be difficult at times. Feelings are often stored in other parts of the body besides the brain. This activity is designed to help you develop an awareness of where information is stored in your body.

METHOD: Every day for a week, stop occasionally and notice how you feel. Where in your body are there sensations (tightness, aches, tickles, temperature changes, etc.) Over the course of the week, use the following chart to note what emotions are attached to these sensations. Add additional emotions to the bottom. Remember, THERE IS NO WRONG WAY TO FEEL!

EMOTION	AREA OF BODY	M	T	W	TH	F	SAT	SUN
PLEASURE								
JOY								
HAPPINESS								
LOVE								
EXCITEMENT								
SEXUAL DESIRE								
PLAYFULNESS								
SADNESS								
GRIEF								
LONELINESS								
BETRAYAL								
NEED								
CONFUSION								
EMBARRASSMENT								
NERVOUSNESS								
ANGER								
FEAR								
IRRITATION								
FRUSTRATION								
HOSTILITY								

Unit Three: Activities for Self-Discovery

1. Which ones did you experienced the most frequently? Why?

2. Where did you sense them in your body and why?

3. What have you learned about the way you experience feelings in your body?

THE FEELING PERSON'S SURVEY

Understanding that we are "emotional beings" and that self-concept is directly tied to how we "feel" about ourselves is a step toward greater self awareness. This activity is designed to help you explore your emotional patterns in your daily relationships. Use the following scale to best represent your reactions:

SCALE: 1: Never
           2: Rarely
           3: Sometimes
           4: Usually
           5: Always

1.	I FEEL MY EMOTIONS AS THEY OCCUR	1	2	3	4	5
2.	I FEEL CONTROLLED BY OUTSIDE FORCES	1	2	3	4	5
3.	I AM IN TOUCH WITH WHAT I WANT	1	2	3	4	5
4.	I EXPRESS POSITIVE EMOTIONS OPENLY	1	2	3	4	5
5.	I AM AWARE ABOUT HOW I FEEL ABOUT OTHERS	1	2	3	4	5
6.	I AM AWARE ABOUT HOW OTHERS PERCEPTIONS AFFECT ME	1	2	3	4	5
7.	I MAKE POSITIVE STATEMENTS ABOUT MYSELF	1	2	3	4	5
8.	I TRY TO CONTROL MY FEELINGS AS MUCH AS POSSIBLE	1	2	3	4	5
9.	I DWELL ON THE PAST OR WORRY ABOUT THE FUTURE	1	2	3	4	5
10.	I AM CONCERNED WITH HOW OTHERS VIEW ME	1	2	3	4	5
11.	I FEEL CONTROLLED BY INTERNAL FORCES	1	2	3	4	5
12.	I AVOID NEGATIVE OR PAINFUL FEELINGS	1	2	3	4	5
13.	I SAY NEGATIVE THINGS TO MYSELF	1	2	3	4	5
14.	I AM AWARE OF HOW MY PAST AFFECTS MY CURRENT REACTIONS	1	2	3	4	5
15.	DAYDREAMS AND FANTASIES ARE AN ESCAPE FOR ME	1	2	3	4	5
16.	I ACCEPT COMPLIMENTS FREELY	1	2	3	4	5
17.	I BELIEVE THAT MY THOUGHTS ARE UNIMPORTANT	1	2	3	4	5
18.	I AM AWARE OF ANY TENSION IN MY BODY	1	2	3	4	5
19.	NEW EXPERIENCES ARE DIFFICULT FOR ME	1	2	3	4	5
20.	I BELIEVE PEOPLE CARE ABOUT WHAT I THINK	1	2	3	4	5

Unit Three: Activities for Self-Discovery

Answer the following discussion questions:

1. What does your understanding of your feelings tell you about yourself as a communicator?

2. How much control do you feel you have over what you think and do?

3. What feelings are the most difficult for you to deal with? Why?

4. How can you work with your feelings more effectively?

DREAM JOURNALING

GOAL: To keep track of subconscious information that comes from night dreaming.

METHOD: For two weeks keep a "dream journal" Upon awakening, lay quietly and allow any "recollections" (images, fragments, thoughts, feelings or words) to drift into your conscious state. If you can recall any dreams, make note of those as well. Write down whatever you are thinking or remembering before starting the day.

Day 1:

Day 2:

Day 3:

Day 4:

Unit Three: Activities for Self-Discovery

Day 5:

Day 6:

Day 7:

Answer the following questions:

1. What "recollections" (actual dream memory or just the "feeling" it created) was the strongest? Why?

2. Do you see a relationship between any given night's recollection? Explain:

3. Do you see a relationship between any recollections and your "waking" life? Explain:

4. What has your dream life been teaching you recently?

SEVEN DAYS OF KINDNESS

PURPOSE: To learn to give to others in a nurturing way.

PART ONE: For seven days you will only communicate **"kindness."** You **can** express caring, giving and nurturing. You **cannot** express selfish desires or purposefully hurt another. Log your experiences daily, including:

The situations; your behavior, the other person's reaction, and your internal feelings:

DAY 1:

DAY 2:

DAY 3:

DAY 4:

DAY 5:

DAY 6:

DAY 7:

PART TWO: List 15 positive reactions you had during this experience:

PART THREE: Discuss how you will apply this experience to your life:

THREE DAYS OF LOVE

PURPOSE: To learn to give and receive love in a comfortable and unconditional manner.

PART ONE: For three days you will only communicate **"love."** You **can** express joy, support, comfort or any positive emotion. You **cannot** express anger, frustration, hostility, aggressiveness or any other **negative emotion.** Log your experiences daily, including:

The situations; your behavior, the other person's reaction, and your internal feelings:

Day 1:

Day 2:

Day 3

Unit Three: Activities for Self-Discovery

PART TWO: In the space below, please discuss the 10 most positive reactions you have to this experience.

PART THREE: Discuss how you will apply this experience to your life:

BIBLIOGRAPHY

Benson, Dr. Herbert, *The Relaxation Response*, Avon Books, NY, 1976.

Bois, Samuel J., *The Art of Awareness*, 3rd Ed., William C. Brown Co. Publishers, Dubuque, IA, 1978.

Bry, Adelaide, *Visualization–Directing the Moves of Your Mind*, Harper & Row, 1978.

Buscaglia, Leo, *Born For Love*, Slack Inc., New Jersey, 1992.

California State Department of Education, "Toward a State of Esteem: The Final Report of the California Task Force to Promote Self-Esteem and Personal and Social Responsibility," *Bureau of Publications, California*, 1990.

———, "Campus TM Seen as I.Q. Booster," *Brain/Mind Bulletin*, January, 1992, pp. 1.

Canfield, Jack, "Wholistic Education in the New Age," *Mind: Evolution or Revolution? TheEmergence of Holistic Education*, Holistic Education Network, Del Mar, CA, 1980.

Canfield, Jack and Wells, Harold, *100 Ways to Enhance Self-Concept in the Classroom*, Prentice-Hall Publishers, Englewood Cliffs, NJ, 1976.

Cartwright, Rosalind, Ph.D., and Lynne Lamberg, "Directing Your Dreams," *Psychology Today*, November/December, 1992, pp. 32–86.

Chopra, Deepak, *Quantum Healing*, Bantam Books, New York, 1989.

Clarke, Jean, *Self-Esteem: A Family Affair*, Harper Collins Publisher, 1978.

Coleman, Wim and Pat Perrin, Ed., *Marilyn Ferguson's PragMagic*, Pocket Books, New York, 1991.

Unit Three: Activities for Self-Discovery

Covey, Stephen R., *The 7 Habits of Highly Effective People*, Simon & Schuster, Inc., New York, 1989.

DePorter, Bobbi and Hernacki, Mike, *Quantum Learning*, Dell Publishing, NY, 1992.

Dervlany, John, "To Sleep......," *Seventeen Magazine*, January, 1993, pp. 84.

Diamond, Dr. John, *Your Body Doesn't Lie*, Harper & Row Publishers, Inc., NY, 1979.

Elkins, Dov Peretz, *Glad To Be Me: Building Self-Esteem In Yourself and Others*, Prentice-Hall, Englewood Cliffs, NJ, 1976.

Epstein, David and Karen Johnston, "Impress Your Friends! Stagger Your Colleagues? Here's Twenty Terrific Brain Facts to Spruce Up Your Next Conversation!" *Your Personal Best*, Rodale Press, September, 1991, Vol. 3, No. 9, pp. 12–13.

Evatt, Cris, *He & She: 60 Significant Differences Between Men and Women*, Conari Press, Berkley, CA 1992.

Fields, Rick, Peggy Taylor, Rex Weyler and Rick Ingrasci, *Chop Wood, Carry Water*, Jeremy P. Tarcher, Inc., Los Angeles, 1984.

————, "Female Attention Can Be Healthy," *Your Personal Best*, August, 1990, pp. 5.

Freedman, Rita, *Bodylove: Learning to Like Our Looks—and Ourselves*, Harper & Row, New York, 1988.

Gardner, Howard, *Frames of Mind*, Basic Books Incorporated Publishers, NY, 1985.

Garfield, Patricia, "The Healing Power of Dreams," *New Age Journal*, June, 1991, pp. 34–41.

Gillett, Richard, "Be a Positive Thinker," *New Woman Magazine*, K–III Magazine Corporation, August, 1992, pp. 50–53.

Goleman, Daniel, Paul Coffman and Michael Ray, *The Creative Spirit*, Penguin Group, NY, 1992.

Goleman, Daniel, "Type T—New Risk Taking," *Self*, March 1991, pp. 133–186.

Halpern, Steve, *Sound Health*, Harper & Row, San Francisco, 1985.

Harris, Anastas, Ed., *Mind: Evolution or Revolution? The Emergence of Holistic Education*, The Holistic Education Network, Del Mar, CA, 1980.

Hooper, Judith and Teresi, Dick, *The 3-Pound Universe*, Dell Publishing, NY, 1986.

Jeffers, Susan, Ph.D., *Feel the Fear and Do It Anyway*, Fawcett Columbine, New York, 1987.

Joudry, Patricia, *Sound Therapy for the Walkman*, Steele and Steele Publishers, Dalmeny, Canada, 1984.

Keller, Fred, "Television and the Slow Death of the Mind," *Communication Probes*, 3rd Ed., Science Research Associates, 1982, pp. 83–91.

King, Viki, *Beyond Visualization*, New World Library, San Rafael, CA 1992.

Klinger, Eric, Ph.D., "Daydreams: What They Can Do For You," *New Realities*, January/February, 1991, pp. 8–13.

Lawren, Bill, "The Older Brain—Still Creative After All These Years," *Good Housekeeping*, November, 1992.

Lawrence, Gordon, *People Types & Tiger Stripes*, Center for Applications of Psychological Type, Inc., Gainsville, FL, 1979.

Levine, Barbara, *Your Body Believes Every Word You Say*, Aslan Publishing, Boulder Creek, CA 1991.

Litvak, Stuart, *Use Your Head*, Prentice-Hall Publishers, Englewood Cliffs, NJ, 1982.

Livermore, Beth, "Build a Better Brain," *Psychology Today*, Sussex Publishers Inc., September/October, 1992, pp. 40–47.

Loch, Chuck, "How to Feed Your Brain and Develop Your Creativity," *Writer's Digest*, February, 1981, PP. 20–23.

Mortenson, David, *Communication, The Study of Human Interaction*, Kingsport Press, Inc.,1972, pp. 78.

Myers, David G., "The Secrets of Happiness," *Psychology Today*, Sussex Publishers Inc., July/August, 1992, pp. 38–45.

Myers, David G., *The Pursuit of Happiness: Who is Happy—And Why?*, William Morrow, Inc., NY, 1992.

Sally Olds, "Days of Solitude", *New Woman Magazine*, May, 1992, pp. 58.

Ostrander, Sheila, and Lynn Schroeder, *Super-Memory: The Revolution*, Carroll & Graff Publishers, Inc., New York, 1991.

Oyle, Dr. Irvine, *The Healing Mind*, Celestial Arts Publishing, Millbrae, CA, 1975.

Patel, Rahul, "Healing Mind and Body," *Body, Mind, Spirit*, January/February, 1992, pp. 50–51.

Peterson, Susan, "The Dream Machine," *The Orange County Register*, March, 13, 1991.

Reps, Paul, *10 Ways To Meditate*, Walker and Weatherhill Publishing Co., NY, 1969.

————, "Retrospective: Unlocking the Mystery of Creativity," *Brain/Mind Bulletin*, September, 1990, pp. 2.

————, "Right Brain Edge," *Brain/Mind Bulletin*, March 1991, pp. 2.

Ruben, David, "Meditation Breaks Into the Mainstream," *New Age Journal Magazine*, May/June, 1991, pp. 46.

Rubenstein, Carin, "The New Woman's Report on Self-Esteem," *New Woman Magazine*, K–III Magazine Corporation, October, 1992, pp. 58–66.

Russell, Peter, *The Brain Book*, Penguin Books, NY, 1979.

Ryan, Regina Sara and John W. Travis, M.D., *Wellness: Small Changes You Can Use to Make a Big Difference*, Ten Speed Press, Berkley, CA, 1991.

Samples, Bob, Cheryl Charles, Dick Barnhart, *The Whole School Book*, Addison/Wesley Publishing, Reading, MA, 1977.

Samuels, Mike, M.D. and Nancy Samuels, *Seeing With the Mind's Eye*, Random House, New York, 1975.

Siegel, Bernie, M.D., *Love, Medicine and Miracles*, Harper & Rowe, NY, 1986.

Siegel, Lee, "You Can Dream Your Way to New Skills, Scientist Finds," *Orange County Register*, October, 28, 1992., pp. 1.

Sky, Michael, *Breathing*, Bear and Co., Publishing, Sante Fe, NM, 1990.

Stevens, John O., *Awareness: Exploring, Experimenting, Experiencing*, Bantam, NY, 1973.

Strong, Polly, *Thirteen Authorities Tell You What Your Dreams Mean*, Berkley Books, NY, 1990.

Syer, John, Connelly, Christopher, *Sporting Body, Sporting Mind*, Prentice-Hall Publishing, Englewood Cliffs, NJ, 1989.

Tame, Dr. David, *The Secret Power of Music*, Destiny Books, Rochester, VT, 1984.

Tein, Joseph, M.F.C.C., "Focusing," *Better World*, Vol. 1, No. 3, pp. 24–22.

————, "Toward a State of Self-Esteem," *New Woman*, March, 1991, pp.54–57.

Tyler, Augin, "Optimists Considered Better Equipped To Battle Stress," *Santa Ana Register*.

Ungerleider, Steven, Ph.D., "Visions of Victory," *Psychology Today*, Sussex Publishers, Inc., July/August, 1992, pp. 46–53.

Urbanska, Wanda, "Self-Esteem: The Hope of the Future," *New Woman Magazine*, K–III Magazine Corporation, March, 1991, pp. 52–58.

Vasconcellos, John, "Education For What?" *Mind: Evolution or Revolution? The Emergence of Holistic Education,* Holistic Education Network, Del Mar, CA, 1980.

Williams, Linda Verlee, *Teaching for the Two-Sided Mind,* Prentice-Hall Publishing, New Jersey, 1983.

Wood, Stephanie, "Relax," *McCall's,* July, 1991, pp. 50.

Zukav, Gary, *Dancing Wu Li Masters,* Wm. Morrow & Co., Inc., NY, 1979.

INDEX

Index

Index

Index

Index

Index